YORK FILM NOTES

Some Like It Hot

Director
Billy Wilder

Note by Lorraine Rolston

York Press
Longman

York Press
322 Old Brompton Road, London SW5 9JH

Pearson Education Limited
Edinburgh Gate, Harlow, Essex CM20 2JE, United Kingdom
Associated companies, branches and representatives throughout the world

First published 2000

ISBN 0-582-40503-3

Designed by Vicki Pacey
Phototypeset by Gem Graphics, Trenance, Mawgan Porth, Cornwall
Colour reproduction and film output by Spectrum Colour
Printed in Malaysia, KVP

contents

author of this note Lorraine Rolston has a Masters degree in film studies from Sheffield Hallam University. She is a former film reviewer for Manchester's *City Life* magazine. She is currently the Cinemas Education Officer at Cornerhouse in Manchester.

background

trailer

Some Like It Hot is a wacky, clever, farcical comedy that starts off like a firecracker and keeps on throwing off lively sparks till the very end.

Variety

As the band's somewhat simple singer/ukulele player, Miss Monroe, whose figure simply cannot be overlooked, contributes more assets than the obvious ones to this madcap romp. As a pushover for gin and the tonic effect of saxophone players, she sings a couple of whispery old numbers ('Running Wild' and 'I Wanna Be Loved By You') and also proves to be the epitome of a dumb blonde and a talented comedienne.

A.H. Weiler, The New York Times

Marilyn does herself proud, giving a performance of such intrinsic quality that you begin to believe she's only being herself and it is herself who fits into that distant period and this picture so well.

Archer Winston, The New York Post

Most of Billy Wilder's new piece – a farce blacker than is common on the American screen – whistles along at a smart, murderous pace.

critic Dilys Powell

A comedy set in the Prohibition era, with transvestism, impotence, role confusion, and borderline inversion – and all hilariously innocent, though always on the brink of really disastrous double-entendre.

critic Pauline Kael

a performance of melting charm

> The wit, speed and zest of the movie lose nothing with the passing of time. During the making of the film Monroe was at her most difficult and tiresome ... but the result – a performance of melting charm – was worth it.
>
> *Barry Norman, 100 Best Films of the Century*

> Before it was completed and released, *Some Like It Hot* was considered a joke in the industry – many people thinking it was a ludicrous endeavour with an asinine plot, a sure failure.
>
> *actor Jack Lemmon*

> You want machine guns and dead bodies and gags in the same picture? Forget about it Billy, you'll never make it work.
>
> *film producer, David O. Selznick*

reading some like it hot

Some Like It Hot is one of the greatest film comedies of all time. First released in 1959, it was directed by Billy Wilder, and stars Marilyn Monroe, Tony Curtis and Jack Lemmon. It is now part of Hollywood legend – not least because of Marilyn Monroe's on-set reputation. Made for United Artists at a cost of 2.8 million dollars, it came in at 500,000 dollars over budget – a considerable sum now, and far more so then. It was the third-biggest box-office hit of 1959 and earned 7 million dollars that year alone.

The film's success is attributable to a clever combination of its many contrasting elements. In the melting pot are 1920s gangster movies (with period costumes, feuding gangs and speakeasies); a sustained joke about entangled identities and cross-dressing; heaps of slapstick comedy; and last but certainly not least, Marilyn Monroe. At one and the same time it harks back to the film comedies of the 1930s – the classics from the Marx Brothers and Mack Sennett – and addresses changes in attitudes to sexuality that would grow widespread in the dawning 1960s.

It was nominated for six Academy Awards, or 'Oscars', including Best Director for Billy Wilder, Best Actor for Jack Lemmon and Best Adapted

rechristened 'Josephine' and 'Daphne'

Screenplay. Perhaps surprisingly, the only winner was Orry Kelly, for Best Costume Design (Black and White), at a time when Best Costume (Colour) was still a separate award.

Some Like It Hot is set in America in 1929 – the Prohibition era. The action begins in Chicago, where gangland violence is rife, before moving on to the sunnier climes of Miami. Joe and Jerry are a pair of musicians, playing sax and bass respectively, making a meagre living performing at illegal drinking parties. When one of the venues is raided, they find themselves out of work. The Depression is also getting under way, and jobs are thin on the ground, but they manage to land one night's work. On the way there they witness a bloody massacre – the work of Chicago's chief mobster Spats Colombo (George Raft). Knowing that the gang will dispense with all witnesses, Joe and Jerry take desperate steps. Donning high heels and make-up, they hotfoot it out of town to the only job they find – as members of Sweet Sue and Her Society Syncopators, a sassy, all-girl jazz band. Rechristened 'Josephine' and 'Daphne', they join the band on a train bound for Florida. On board they meet Sugar 'Kane' Kowalczyk (Marilyn Monroe), the band's singer and ukulele player. Joe immediately falls for Sugar, and on arriving in Florida, he disguises himself yet again – this time as a millionaire, in order to win her favour. Meanwhile, Daphne attracts a real millionaire of her own – Osgood Fielding III (Joe E. Brown).

The script was written by director Billy Wilder, with his long-term writing companion, I.A.L. Diamond – with a working title of *Not Tonight Josephine!* The original source material was a 1932 German film, *Fanfaren der Liebe* (*Fanfares of Love*), written by Robert Thoeren. This earlier film concerned two musicians so desperate for work they put on various disguises to get jobs in different bands.

I.A.L. Diamond was convinced that in their version, the main characters would need a much stronger motivation to dress as women. The writing partners sought a better approach until Billy Wilder suggested them witnessing the St. Valentine's Day Massacre. He reckoned that with a gang of villains hot on their heels, they would have a good reason to leave town urgently – so urgently that even dressing up as women becomes a plausible option.

like jello on springs

Central to the film's success are the performances of Tony Curtis and Jack Lemmon as the men-turned-women. To help them create believable characters, Billy Wilder chose to shoot the film in black and white, as early colour screen tests of Tony Curtis and Jack Lemmon in drag and make-up made the actors look 'freakish'. This decision created an end result that made them look less ridiculous and more believable to the viewer. Billy Wilder did, however, have to convince Marilyn Monroe that shooting in black and white would be to the film's advantage. Marilyn Monroe had a clause in her contract stating that all of her films had to be in colour. The actress agreed to the director's wishes, and went on to strengthen the production even further by suggesting that her opening scene was weak and needed reworking. Together with Billy Wilder, she altered the scene – which initially showed her simply approaching the train playing her ukulele. The finished version is one of the great screen entrances of all time: Sugar sashays down the platform and does her famous wiggle as she moves to avoid a puff of smoke from the train. Jerry – as Daphne – looks on in amazement, saying, 'Look at that, it's like jello on springs'. This sequence automatically positions Sugar as representative of true femininity – in contrast to Joe and Jerry's pretend women.

There are differing accounts of whom the lead roles were originally written for. Some sources claim that United Artists originally wanted Bob Hope and Danny Kaye as the male leads. Later, they pushed for Frank Sinatra. Such big names dropped off the agenda, though, when Marilyn Monroe expressed an interest: too many big names might have overloaded the film perhaps or, more practically, cost too much and caused ego clashes on set. Initially Billy Wilder and I.A.L. Diamond hadn't envisaged such a starry name as Marilyn playing the part: as Billy Wilder says:

> We just wanted any girl, because it was not such a big part. Mitzi Gaynor was who we had in mind. The word came that Marilyn wanted the part. And then we *had* to have Marilyn. We opened every door to get Marilyn. And we got her.
>
> *Crowe, 1999*

one essential ingredient ... sex

According to Tony Curtis's autobiography, it was agent Lew Wasserman who was influential in bringing Tony Curtis and Jack Lemmon to the picture, seeing the potential of them playing drag.

After *The Seven Year Itch* (1955), Billy Wilder had declared that he would never work with Marilyn Monroe again. Nevertheless, when she read the script of *Some Like It Hot* and wanted to do it, Billy Wilder was delighted, saying, 'She was tough to work with, but what you had, by hook or by crook, once you saw it on the screen it was amazing' (Crowe, 1999). Most crucially though, Marilyn Monroe brought one essential ingredient to the film: sex.

Although her presence was initially warmly welcomed, both cast and crew would soon regret her involvement with the film. She began to live up to her reputation as a 'difficult' performer: consistently showing up late, forgetting her lines, and spending an endless amount of time in her dressing room. There are many accounts of her erratic behaviour and of the problems that she created on the set. Billy Wilder took to writing out her lines on set furniture in the hope that it would get her through her scenes, but even this effort failed. She frequently needed take after take to get her lines right. Billy Wilder says:

> Just a little line, like 'Where's that bourbon?' – she couldn't get it. That was eighty takes or something. You have to remember, when a man muffs a line, and they do it again and again and again, then you replace him, because he plays a small part. Marilyn was the star. She does the takes because it's gonna be in the picture.
>
> *Crowe, 1999*

(The 'Where's the bourbon?' line was eventually written for Marilyn Monroe on the inside of a drawer, and her back is to the camera in the chosen shot.) Marilyn Monroe's behaviour was never consistent however, and at other times she had no problems at all in remembering her lines, as Billy Wilder goes on to say:

> I just remember that we had about fifty-plus takes, and there was the whole afternoon trying to get it, because she cried after every

> take ... Then again – later, for instance, in the scene on the beach with Tony Curtis in the blazer and cap, where he is the co-owner of Shell Oil – there she had a three-page dialogue scene which we had to get quickly because there were marine planes taking off at ten-minute intervals – she got it the first take.
>
> *Crowe, 1999*

Billy Wilder and I.A.L. Diamond had a strict rule never to reveal who wrote which lines in their scripts. But in the case of *Some Like It Hot*, Billy Wilder made an exception. Joe E. Brown's famous last line, 'Well, nobody's perfect', was, he admitted, written by I.A.L. Diamond.

> That was a temporary line, suggested by Mr Diamond. And it wound up to be our funniest last line. I was asked by many people, 'What is going to happen now? What happens now to Lemmon, what happens to his husband?' And I always said, 'I have no idea.' 'Nobody's perfect.' Leave it up there on the screen. You cannot top that.
>
> *Crowe, 1999*

key players' biographies

BILLY WILDER

Director Billy Wilder was one of the foremost film directors of the 1950s – if not of all time. His distinctive style leans towards comedy, often with a dark satirical streak.

Born a Jew in Vienna 1906, Billy Wilder was forced to leave his homeland with the rise of Hitler in the 1930s. He had already begun a career as a screenwriter in collaboration with independent film-makers in Berlin. His destination now was America, where – despite a poor grasp of English – he dreamt of becoming a successful Hollywood screenwriter and, eventually, a director.

His American movie career took off when he began a scriptwriting partnership with Charles Brackett. This urbane and refined man, a former

a string of box-office hits

theatre critic, contrasted well with Billy Wilder. Together they wrote several acclaimed screenplays including *Ninotchka* (1939) and *Ball of Fire* (1941). In 1941 the second of Billy Wilder's ambitions was fulfilled. Paramount assigned him as director on the Ginger Rogers vehicle *The Major and the Minor*. Unusually, though, Billy Wilder continued to co-write all of his films. His partnership with Charles Brackett was put on hold when he made *Double Indemnity* (1944), a powerful film noir co-written with novelist Raymond Chandler. This was released to massive acclaim; Billy Wilder's stock was rising.

The dark tone of *Double Indemnity* also ran through *Sunset Boulevard* (1950). Again written with Charles Brackett, this blistering critique of the Hollywood system starred former silent movie star Gloria Swanson – poignantly as a faded movie star. A host of classic Hollywood names appear: director Erich von Stroheim is Max the butler; Cecil B. De Mille takes on a cameo role, and Buster Keaton appears playing a card game with a number of stars from yesteryear. *Sunset Boulevard* won Billy Wilder acclaim from critics and audiences; he followed it with a string of box-office hits throughout the 1950s, including *Ace in the Hole* (1951) and *Stalag 17* (1953). All contained a dark, edgy streak within the comedy. *Stalag 17* takes place in a German prisoner of war camp (Billy Wilder's mother had been a victim of the Holocaust).

Billy Wilder made both *Sabrina* (1954) and *Love in the Afternoon* (1957) with the petite Audrey Hepburn before finding a new and very different leading lady in the shape of Marilyn Monroe. In *The Seven Year Itch* (1955), Marilyn Monroe appears as a nameless figure of male fantasy, who plagues and entrances a married man, alone without his family over the course of a New York summer. The film turned Monroe the star into Marilyn the legend, encapsulated in one scene: standing above a subway vent, a blast of air from a passing train causes her skirt to billow up around her waist, much to her delight (see Contexts: Stars).

Despite troubled experiences during the making of *The Seven Year Itch*, the director recognised Marilyn Monroe's comic abilities. Come *Some Like It Hot* in 1959, he gladly cast her as Sugar Kane. By this time, he had a wealth of talent to draw on. Scripted with his new writing partner, I.A.L. Diamond a partnership that was to last twenty-four years

(their writing partnership came to eclipse even that with Charles Brackett), it would be the first of many Billy Wilder films to star Jack Lemmon. Billy Wilder would reward Jack Lemmon for playing the part of a man in drag in *Some Like It Hot* by offering him the role of C.C. Baxter in *The Apartment* (1960). Ostensibly a comedy in which C.C. Baxter allows his superiors to conduct their extramarital affairs in his flat, the film also satirises soul-destroying corporate America. Jack Lemmon was nominated for an Oscar for the role.

Billy Wilder's later films include *Irma La Douce* (1963) and *Avanti!* (1972). Although his style remained instantly recognisable, he never performed better at the box office than with *Some Like It Hot*. As audiences grew smaller and the film industry changed (see Contexts: Production), Billy Wilder made fewer and fewer films. A staple in his heyday of the 1950s, by the early 1980s he was an anachronism. After making *Buddy Buddy* in 1981, Billy Wilder retired from film-making.

I.A.L. DIAMOND

I.A.L. Diamond was born in Romania, 1920, as Itek Dominici – although he liked to claim his superfluous initials stood for Interscholastic Algebra League. His career as a Hollywood screenwriter began in 1944, with *Murder in the Blue Room*. By 1957 he was the credited writer of fourteen films: at which point director Billy Wilder saw and admired the material he wrote for a Writer's Guild dinner. I.A.L. Diamond was promptly engaged to co-write *Love in the Afternoon*. This was the start of a partnership that was to last twenty-four years, taking in *Some Like It Hot*, *The Apartment*, *Cactus Flower* (1969) and *Buddy Buddy*.

Wilder-Diamond screenplays are Hollywood classics. Their sparkling dialogue and charming inspired characters won them great acclaim. Three screenplays were nominated for Academy Awards, with *The Apartment* winning for them in 1960. I.A.L. Diamond is also credited as associate producer on seven of the twelve pictures that they wrote together, reflecting the work that he put in on set. His first such credit was on *Some Like It Hot*. I.A.L. Diamond died in Beverly Hills in 1988.

MARILYN MONROE

'I knew we were mid-flight and there was a nut on the plane' – Billy Wilder.

Amongst film critics and fans, *Some Like It Hot* is considered Marilyn Monroe's best performance. The critics responded with delight to Sugar Kane, with even her detractors acknowledging her comic genius and skill in sending up the dumb blonde stereotype she had made so famous.

Born Norma Jean Baker in Los Angeles, California in 1926, she had a traumatic start in life. Accounts of her youth paint a picture of parental neglect and sexual abuse. She spent many of her formative years in orphanages and foster homes. At the age of 16, she married Jim Dougherty, a friend of her guardian. The marriage lasted four years. During this time, a photographer spotted her model potential as she was working in a parachute factory.

Her subsequent career as a successful photographic model led to a 125-dollar-a-week contract with Twentieth Century Fox Studios. Her hair dyed, her name changed, she metamorphosed into Marilyn Monroe – only to be dropped by the studio soon after. Fox were to reassess this decision after Marilyn Monroe received favourable reviews for her roles in *The Asphalt Jungle* (1950) and *All About Eve* (1950), eventually signing her for a lucrative seven-year contract.

In 1953, nude photos of Marilyn – taken in 1948 – became *Playboy* magazine's first ever centrefold spread; thereafter Marilyn Monroe's name on a film was reputed to add 500,000 dollars to its gross takings. In 1953 alone Marilyn Monroe made three films which secured her position and cemented her public persona as a 'dumb blonde' – *Niagara, Gentlemen Prefer Blondes* and *How to Marry a Millionaire*.

The following year she made her first film with director Billy Wilder. Adapted from a hit Broadway play, *The Seven Year Itch* (1955) is the story of a married, forty-something man, played by Tom Ewell (who had made the part his own in the stage version). Just as his wife and child go away on summer vacation, Marilyn Monroe moves into the vacant apartment upstairs. The film is an exercise in titillation, with Marilyn Monroe the personification of every male fantasy. During one scene, Marilyn Monroe –

who plays a character simply known as 'the girl' – leans over the balcony towards her male neighbour, informing him that she keeps her underwear in the refrigerator to help keep her cool in the New York heat. This was strong stuff for the mid 1950s, not least because Marilyn Monroe also looks as though she is nude!

The film was also celebrated for the 'skirt-blowing' scene: Marilyn Monroe stands on a walk-over subway vent, and to her delight, gusts from a train passing underneath cause her wide-pleated skirt to billow up around her shoulders. The press dubbed it 'the most interesting, dramatic display since Lady Godiva'. The film was a massive hit.

In 1956, she repeated her male fantasy 'dumb blonde' act to great effect in *Bus Stop*. But between 1955 and her death in 1962, Marilyn Monroe began to push to be taken more seriously as an actor, once saying, 'I'm waiting for that day when the wolf calls will fade and people will come out of the theatre saying, "That little girl can really act"'. This ambition showed in her attendance of the famous New York Actors' Studio. Run by Lee Strasberg, it practised the so-called 'method' style of acting, made famous by the Russian director Constantin Stanislavsky.

Fyodor Dostoevsky's novel *The Brothers Karamazov* was about to be filmed, and Marilyn Monroe was eager to win the part of Grushenka. She failed to, but she began to prefer starring in films adapted from literary works, seeing such projects as meatier. Marilyn Monroe desperately wanted to rid herself of the dumb blonde image that had made her famous, and attempting a more serious style of acting was crucial to making this switch:

> The importance of the acting motif in Monroe's image is that, if acting ability is granted, it is 'proof' of a real, substantive skill or talent, and such a proof shows that she has moved beyond the sex object category.
>
> *Dyer, 1980*

Not all the critics were convinced that they had seen a change in Marilyn Monroe, as this review of *The Prince and The Showgirl* (1957) from a *New York Tribune* critic reveals:

she was driving everybody nuts

> This is a dumb, affable showgirl and nothing more, and Miss Monroe goes through the motions with mirth, childish innocence, squeals of pleasure, pouts of annoyance, eyes big as golf balls, and many a delighted toss of her rounded surfaces.

There are varied accounts of how Marilyn Monroe ended up working with Billy Wilder again. In 1958, she was in a state of depression following a miscarriage. Her third husband, playwright Arthur Miller, suggested it might do her good to make another Billy Wilder comedy, after the success of *The Seven Year Itch*. Other accounts suggest that she took the part to help pay her husband's substantial legal fees, as he countered the House Un-American Activities witch-hunt (see Contexts: Cultural contexts).

Whatever her motives, Marilyn Monroe went to Hollywood to make the film, although with reservations: she was pregnant again, possibly accounting for some of the problems she caused on the set. Tony Curtis certainly had his fair share of problems with her, as Jack Lemmon recalls:

> Tony had his hands full with Marilyn. She was ill at the time, but we didn't know that until later. All we knew then was that she was driving everybody nuts. You might do fairly long takes with Marilyn, or you might do one, and Billy's gonna print the one that's best for her. I figured that out fairly easily and made up my mind, if I let this get to me, it's going to hurt my performance. But it was easier for me, especially in the second half, because I'm off with a rose in my mouth doing tangos with Joe E. Brown, while Tony has those long scenes with Marilyn.
>
> *Curtis and Paris, 1994*

One comment Tony Curtis made about Marilyn was in response to a reporter asking him what it was like to kiss her: 'It was like kissing Hitler' was his famous reply, which he later said was misinterpreted. 'Somebody asked me what it was like making love to Marilyn, and I said, "what do you want me to say? It was like kissing Hitler".'

untimely death, aged just thirty-six

Marilyn Monroe's own befuddled response to this surfaced in an interview with Richard Merryman from *Life* magazine. Asked about the comment from Tony Curtis, she replied, 'That's his problem ... it's not him, it's somebody else, out with him, get somebody else'. (By the time of this interview, Marilyn Monroe's life was almost over, and drink and drugs were taking their toll.)

Twelve hours after *Some Like It Hot* wrapped, Marilyn Monroe lost the baby. More upset followed, when her marriage to Arthur Miller ended just one week before the release of her last completed film, *The Misfits*. Written especially for her by Arthur Miller, Roslyn in *The Misfits* was to be her only real dramatic role. The film also starred Montgomery Clift and Clark Gable. Clark Gable had famously joked that working with Marilyn Monroe would give him a heart attack. Just two weeks after the film was completed the actor died – of a heart attack. Marilyn Monroe's last job on the unfinished *Something's Got To Give* was short-lived, with her unreliability reaching new heights. She was absent from work a number of times during the thirty-three day shoot. Marilyn Monroe was fired from the film, and just one month later was found dead at her home in a suburb of Los Angeles. The post-mortem concluded that she had taken her own life through an overdose of drugs.

During her lifetime, Marilyn Monroe had allegedly engaged in love affairs with the US president John F. Kennedy and his brother Robert. After her death, conspiracy theories abounded that foul play from on high had been involved in her demise. Despite her untimely death, aged just thirty-six, Marilyn Monroe had made a total of thirty films, ensuring her status as a screen icon and star of legendary proportions (see Contexts: Stars).

TONY CURTIS

'I would be happy if I could equal his career and his lasting power' – Tony Curtis on his idol, Cary Grant.

Tony Curtis was born Bernard Schwartz in 1925 in New York City, the son of a Hungarian immigrant. With his rebel appeal, early studio publicity presented him as a juvenile delinquent. During a Greenwich Village production of *Golden Boy* a talent scout saw him, spotted his potential and recommended him to Universal. He secured a seven-year contract with Universal – at the time one of the largest studios, who trained young actors and actresses in the rudiments of an acting career, offering classes in voice, dramatics and so on. The young Tony Curtis made an unbilled debut in *Criss Cross* in 1948, and went on to have small parts in a number of other films before hitting the big time.

Tony Curtis was a fan-magazine editor's dream and Universal exploited his looks to the full in their early marketing of the potential star. At one point the studio claimed to be receiving up to 10,000 fan letters a week. Tony Curtis's slicked-back, mean and moody look was enormously influential: in 1951, a sixteen-year-old boy from northern Mississippi changed his hairstyle to what he called a 'Tony Curtis cut'. The boy, Elvis Presley, went on to make the look his own.

Tony Curtis has starred in almost one hundred films, among the early ones, *City Across the River* (1949), *Sweet Smell of Success* (1957) and *The Vikings* (1958). He played opposite Burt Lancaster in *Trapeze*, and by 1957 he was earning 25,000 dollars a week.

Whilst he was making *Houdini* (1953) at Paramount, Tony Curtis's talents caught the eye of Billy Wilder. When the time came to cast *Some Like It Hot* in 1958, Billy Wilder earmarked Tony Curtis for the role of Joe. 'I was sure Tony was right for it', explains Billy Wilder, 'because he was quite handsome, and when he tells Marilyn Monroe that he is one of the Shell Oil family, she has to be able to believe it' (Curtis and Paris, 1994).

Known as a rebellious, macho matinée idol, it was a brave career move for Tony Curtis to accept the part: he spends much of the film in full drag as Josephine. Notoriously, Billy Wilder provided coaching for Tony Curtis and Jack Lemmon in the form of a female impersonator named Barbette. Barbette's verdict ran: 'Tony is wonderful ... Lemmon is totally impossible' (Curtis and Paris, 1994).

Essentially cast as the straight man to Jack Lemmon's comedian (although in initial discussions, Tony Curtis was to star with Frank Sinatra), Tony Curtis does well to avoid obvious pitfalls: Joe is an attractive, engaging character, and in his twin disguises Tony Curtis manages to create comedy of his own. The actor himself has expressed mixed feelings about the role, however.

> I never felt secure on *Some Like It Hot.* It had nothing to do with Jack [Lemmon]. It was that almost all my scenes were aimed in Marilyn's or Jack's direction. I was the straight man for both of them. I was disappointed.
>
> *Curtis and Paris, 1994*

There was also friction with Marilyn Monroe: her erratic nature frayed nerves on set, leading Tony Curtis to dub her 'Hitler'.

Nevertheless, Tony Curtis's performance is strong and well loved. His dabbling in cross-dressing comedy didn't harm his career at all: poetically, his next film – *Operation Petticoat* (1959) – saw him co-starring with his idol, Cary Grant. Tony Curtis's later films include *Spartacus* (1960), and *The Boston Strangler* (1968). He appears as 'the Senator' in *Insignificance* (1985): although not named, Tony Curtis's role approximates US Senator McCarthy; whilst co-star Theresa Russell's 'Actress' is clearly modelled on Marilyn Monroe. Tony Curtis remains a Hollywood legend.

JACK LEMMON

'Happiness', said Billy Wilder, 'is working with Jack Lemmon'.

Born, as John Uhler Lemmon III, to a lower-middle-class family in Boston in 1925, 'Jack' today has starred in over forty films. *Some Like It Hot* was only the eleventh, and so came relatively early in his long acting career. He was a junior officer in the navy until the end of the war, studying simultaneously at Harvard, focusing on dramatics. His career was kick-started on moving to New York to study acting. Roles in radio soap operas led to a stack of television work – 'I must have done five hundred live shows in New York in two or three years' – and eventually Broadway drama.

The head of Columbia spotted him on television and cast him in his first film role, as Pete Shepherd, opposite Judy Holliday, in *It Should Happen To You* (1954). The film was to set him up as 'the desperate sincere young man, a bit naïve, very good hearted, always game but liable to panic' (Baltake, 1986). Columbia's publicity for the film introduced Jack Lemmon as simply 'a guy you're gonna like'. Jack Lemmon's star was in the ascendant. His name was getting known, as the public grew fond of his comic talents and human, often harassed quality. By the time of *Operation Mad Ball* (1957), he was receiving star billing.

Still, Jack Lemmon wasn't in the same star-league as Marilyn Monroe. When the leading lady agreed to lend her talents to *Some Like It Hot*, and a lesser-known name was required as a co-star, Jack Lemmon, with his appealing knack for comedy, was ideal. It is notable, too, that Jack Lemmon as a name wasn't on a par with Tony Curtis either: the latter had been star material for a couple of years by this point.

Nevertheless, Jack Lemmon's winning performance as Jerry won him a legion of fans: not least Billy Wilder, who resolved to Jack Lemmon, 'Someday, I'm gonna write a role especially for you.' Sure enough, Billy Wilder's next film, *The Apartment*, starred Jack Lemmon as insurance clerk C.C. Baxter, and both received Academy Award nominations; Billy Wilder won in his category. This working partnership continued through *Irma la Douce*, *The Fortune Cookie* (1966), *Avanti!*, *The Front Page* (1974), and *Buddy, Buddy*. 'He was my Everyman', declared Billy Wilder, 'and he could do everything – except carry a love interest.'

Jack Lemmon's wider acting career became, if anything, more successful after *Some Like It Hot*. In *Pepe* (1960), he took a fleeting cameo in full Daphne get-up: in 1964, he was voted Number 1 Male Box-Office Star in America. Over time, he increasingly chose dramatic parts: in 1973 he received an Academy Award for his role as Harry in the thoughtful *Save the Tiger*.

Jack Lemmon's best-known role, though, is undeniably comic: as Felix opposite Walter Matthau's Oscar in *The Odd Couple* (1968). This adaptation of Neil Simon's play pits the pair against one another as ill-tempered housemates. The partnership stuck: Jack Lemmon continues to work to this day, and recently re-teamed with Matthau for *Grumpy Old Men* (1993), the sequel Grumpier Old *Men* (1995) and a belated *Odd Couple II* (1998).

the biggest mouth in the world

JOE E. BROWN

Joseph Even Brown was born in Ohio in 1892. By the age of ten he was part of a touring vaudeville act, as one of the Five Marvellous Ashtons, a tumbling team. As a young man he honed his performing skills in circuses and vaudeville shows, and in 1929 signed a film contract with Warner Brothers studios. Joe E. Brown's distinctive features became familiar to movie-goers, and he won a loyal following. He rose to the heights of comic master in a series of Warner Brothers films in the 1930s, most famously *Elmer the Great* (1933) and *Alibi Ike* (1935) – both with a baseball setting.

By the late 1950s, Joe E. Brown's career had faltered: a string of his films had been poorly received, and roles grew less frequent. Nevertheless, today's audiences know him best for one of these occasional later performances – as Osgood Fielding III in *Some Like It Hot* – rather than for his earlier work. Billy Wilder met Joe E. Brown whilst attending an ice hockey game at which he was compèring, just as the film was being cast. Joe E. Brown agreed to do the role straight away, and he was introduced to a whole new audience. Billy Wilder says, 'He was an absolute surprise to people, to young people, because they'd never seen him. He had the biggest mouth in the world. He was the nicest guy' (Crowe, 1999).

Joe E. Brown made just two films after *Some Like It Hot* was completed, before gracefully retiring. He died in 1973.

GEORGE RAFT

George Raft was a smooth, rather sinister leading man who made his name playing gamblers, nightclub dancers and gangsters. After an impoverished start, growing up in New York's Hell's Kitchen, he arrived in Hollywood in the late 1920s. His first major role was in *Scarface* (1932) in which he played the coin-tossing gangster Guino Rinaldo (look out for the reference in *Some Like It Hot* – see Contexts: Intertextuality). In his own life, George Raft was said to keep the company of gangsters; this, coupled with the fact that he brought such a convincing intensity to the roles he played, gave rise to the rumour that he was a gangster himself. Despite the fact that

George Raft had a long career spanning fifty years in Hollywood, by the latter part of his life, his criminal associations had taken him out of the limelight and out of favour with the studios and the public. By the time he made *Some Like It Hot* in 1959, he was reduced to caricaturing the gangster roles he had made his own in films like *Manpower* (1941) and *Each Dawn I Die* (1939). He died in Hollywood in 1980.

PAT O'BRIEN

Another Hollywood star from the studio days, Pat O'Brien chose acting over the priesthood. This didn't deter him from playing the parts of priests on more than one occasion – in fact they were his staple role during his time at Warners. A popular actor during the 1930s and 1940s, Pat O'Brien's biggest claim to fame was co-starring with James Cagney in nine films over five decades, including the classic gangster film, *Angels with Dirty Faces* (1938). When he wasn't playing priests or gangsters, however, he doubled as a fast-talking reporter or a happy-go-lucky adventurer. By the mid 1940s, the parts started to dry up, although he managed to keep on acting, latterly in character roles such as Sergeant Mulligan in *Some Like It Hot.*

director as auteur

Billy Wilder's trademark features include the wit and cynicism of his (and I.A.L. Diamond's) unforgettable dialogue, skilful camerawork, and atmospheric direction. His films are a cross between Hollywood credibility and the more elite arena of the auteur.

Auteur theory is essentially concerned with raising the status of film director to something superior. Analogies with the art world are often drawn upon to provide parallels, suggesting that directors working within the studio system can be compared to artists and composers such as Michelangelo or Mozart, who also had to work within institutional constraints.

Ever since it was first put forward in the 1950s by a group of critics in the French journal *Cahiers du cinéma* (including François Truffaut and Claude Chabrol), auteur theory has occupied a central position within film studies and film theory. The *Cahiers* critics formulated the notion of the director as auteur, claiming that 'in spite of the industrial nature of film production, the director, like any other artist, was the sole author of the finished product' (Lapsley and Westlake, 1994).

In other words, a film's recognisable and significant features are accredited to the vision of the director. Directors cited by the *Cahiers* critics as the great auteurs included Fritz Lang, John Huston, Orson Welles and William Wyler. The master, to them, was Alfred Hitchcock. What fascinated François Truffaut and Claude Chabrol in particular about Alfred Hitchcock was the way he manipulated his characters, blighting them with obsessive guilt, suspicion and fear, whilst also maintaining a steely control over the audience. Essentially what the *Cahiers* critics did was to elevate popular cinema, making it acceptable to study and deconstruct American cinema in a way that had previously been reserved for art, and art cinema.

Auteur theory is about the pleasure of studying cinema: the thrill of recognising the stylistic traits and elements which run between a director's films. Whether or not Billy Wilder can be considered an auteur, there is certainly pleasure to be had in studying and considering the body of his films, and his individual, creative style. Take for instance his choice of character names:

> There was one name, one man that I had in three or four pictures. Always the same type of character. It was a name I liked, you know. The name was Sheldrake. It has little vibes there. It had profile. It's not like Mr Jones or Mr Weber or something.
>
> *Crowe, 1999*

Another of the characteristic traits of Billy Wilder's films are the voice-overs. Voice-overs exist in many of Billy Wilder's best-known films from *Double Indemnity* to William Holden's dark commentary over the top of *Sunset Boulevard*, and the cynicism of Jack Lemmon in *The Apartment*. Billy Wilder favours the voice-over technique, preferring to say in a few seconds what would take six to twelve pages of script, so long as it is not simply stating the obvious:

resembled a husband-and-wife team

> Voice-over is good as long as you are not describing what the audience is already seeing. You don't have to tell them what they're looking at. Show, don't tell.
>
> *Crowe, 1999*

Comedy, the dominant mode of many of Billy Wilder's films, can also be considered a recognisable feature of his work. As with all good comedy, timing is crucial and Billy Wilder knew exactly where to place the joke in a scene and how long to extend it before ending on a high note. In *Some Like It Hot*, after Jerry has been tangoing with Osgood, Daphne returns to Joe and breaks the news that she has got engaged. The scene lasts for around three minutes, during which Billy Wilder times the jokes to match the rhythm of Daphne's maraca-playing. He says,

> I needed some kind of an action that helped the joke. For instance, Tony Curtis comes up. He says, 'Well, what's new here?' then I put in the other straight line, then comes another joke. But I timed it so that not one straight line is lost. Because sometimes you have a straight line and the straight line gets the laugh. So now you're really dead, because they will not hear the payoff. They laughed over the straight line ... the rhythm is off. You have to be very, very careful.
>
> *Crowe, 1999*

Billy Wilder shot his films extraordinarily quickly, making one in as little as forty-five days. Not surprisingly, the scripts were always of necessity tight, typically containing detailed set directions. According to Billy Wilder's wife, Audrey, his working partnership with I.A.L. Diamond resembled a husband-and-wife team. Billy Wilder pitched dialogue whilst I.A.L. Diamond took care of the specifics, policing every line of dialogue, even on set. Although they were script collaborators, Billy Wilder, as director, is the better-known of the two. Billy Wilder, however, believes that I.A.L. Diamond was worthy of recognition for his contribution: 'I was the lead horse, because I also directed. But Diamond absolutely deserves all the credit he can get' (Crowe, 1999).

signature performances

His leading actors and actresses also contributed greatly to the look of Billy Wilder's films. Audrey Hepburn, with her Givency costumes in *Sabrina*; Gloria Swanson's faded glamour in *Sunset Boulevard*; and certainly Marilyn Monroe, all contributed signature performances in his films. Of these actresses, Marilyn Monroe's performances are the ones most readily associated with Billy Wilder's films.

narrative & form

narrative

The plot of *Some Like It Hot* is simple and well honed. Two out-of-work musicians, Joe and Jerry, need to get out of town after witnessing a bloody massacre. Disguised as women, they join an all-girl band and meet the band's singer, Sugar Kane, who wants to find and marry a millionaire. Joe falls for Sugar and, in order to win her over, he disguises himself again, this time as the heir of the Shell Oil fortune.

This brief outline establishes the two major plot lines – getting away from the mob, and getting the girl. As such the film presents itself along conventional patterns, the escape pattern and the romance pattern. Many Hollywood films represent a double causal structure: one strand is typically a romance, whilst the other is usually connected to external factors such as work, battle, etc. The two are usually interdependent – for example Joe and Jerry have to stay dressed as women in order to avoid the mob, but because Joe is in disguise, he can't reveal his true identity to Sugar. Many Hollywood films use multiple protagonists. *Some Like It Hot* has three main players – Joe, Jerry and Sugar. Although early scenes suggest Joe and Jerry are the principal protagonists, the film's opening credit sequence positions Marilyn Monroe's name first, with the implication that hers is the most important character in the film (or at least the biggest star – see Contexts: Stars).

The narrative system employed within *Some Like It Hot* is the classical Hollywood model. Classical Hollywood cinema, also known as classical narrative, is so called because of its long history as the dominant narrative form within the American studio system. The classical narrative model is also referred to as 'realist' cinema, because it gives the appearance of a seamless view of the world. Crucial to this notion of 'realism' is editing. At its simplest, editing can be defined as 'the juxtaposition of individual shots'

a narrative is essentially a story

(Cook, 1994). In classical narrative cinema, editing positions the shots sequentially according to the order of story events, providing the viewer with an easy to read, linear view: 'Continuity editing establishes spatial and temporal relationships between shots in such a way as to permit the spectator to "read" a film without any conscious effort' (Cook, 1994).

Right after the raid at the speakeasy, Joe talks Jerry into hocking their coats and putting the money on a dog which Joe believes to be a favourite, 'He's a shoo-in. I got the word from Max the waiter – his brother-in-law is the electrician who wires the rabbit.' The camera cuts to the next scene, which needs no words to tell us that the dog didn't win, and that Joe and Jerry are without their coats on a snow-covered street in the middle of winter. The next line of dialogue comes from Jerry who says, 'Greased Lightning! Why do I listen to you? I ought to have my head examined.' Thus the editing works to link the two shots in a logical and clever way. Whether we call it mainstream, dominant or classical cinema, we intuitively recognise classical narrative cinema on seeing it.

Classical Hollywood cinema is based around the decisions and choices of individual characters or groups of characters – a character who desires something or someone is often the jumping-off point of any given narrative. In *Some Like It Hot*, Joe and Jerry are desperate to get out of town because they know the mob will soon come looking for them. All that follows comes as a result of this desire.

At its most basic a narrative is essentially a story, one which involves events and characters. The events need some sort of logic, to enable the audience to make sense of the film (unless it is a non-narrative, experimental-style film) and the characters need traits and motivation. Narratives also usually need an ending in order to bring the story to closure, although some films are open-ended, leaving the viewer to make up their own mind about the outcome (usually more of an arthouse tendency than present in mainstream Hollywood movies).

Despite the fact that classical Hollywood structure is easy to follow, the viewer is still constantly interpreting and linking events in order to construct and make sense of the narrative. Often 'red herrings' are present – superfluous information and narrative threads which aren't developed.

narrative

'my spine turns to custard'

All the events presented in a film compose the story. The story world is often referred to as the diegesis – a Greek word meaning 'recounted story'. In the opening scene of *Some Like It Hot*, the cars, dimly lit narrow streets, the speakeasy and the gangsters are all diegetic – that is, they exist within the world of the story. The plot contains elements of the film which are presented to us as 'story': the elements we see and hear as well as those which we infer or assume. Story and plot overlap. The story is the sum total of all the events in the narrative. Some events are presented directly (making them part of the plot) whilst others are merely hinted at or suggested; others are even ignored. We learn from Sugar that she has had a string of unsuccessful love affairs with saxophone players,

You see, I have this thing about saxophone players ... especially tenor sax. I don't know what it is, but they just curdle me. All they have to do is play eight bars of 'Come to Me My Melancholy Baby' – and my spine turns to custard, and I get goose-pimply all over – and I come to them.

Yet we never actually find out anything much about any of the men involved, or meet them, so this aspect of the story lies outside the plot.

One of the skills of narrative cinema is in connecting events. Cause and effect – something happens to cause something else to happen – is the standard means of advancing the plot. Causal motivation and information are often planted in advance of a scene. For example, Sugar likes to drink: she tells Josephine and Daphne almost as soon as they meet her,

I don't want you to think that I'm a drinker. I can stop any time I want to – only I don't want to. Especially when I'm blue.

Just a couple of short scenes later, during the band's rehearsal on the train, a hip flask drops out from underneath Sugar's garter. Jerry covers up for her, leading to a friendship between Sugar and the two new 'girls'.

'I can stop any time I want to'

Sugar tells Josephine and Daphne she can stop drinking 'any time'

places have particular importance

Cause and effect takes place in time. Scenes in classical narrative cinema typically consist of an introduction and an establishing shot which positions the characters in time and space, establishing when the action is happening and where. As characters interact, the scene is broken up into closer views of the action and reaction, whilst lighting, setting, music and so forth all enhance whatever is taking place (see Style). A scene will often close with a shot of a particular portion of space or a significant object, providing the transition from one scene to the next.

We construct story time on the basis of what the plot presents – the plot often presents events out of chronological order. Temporal factors are significant in helping us to construct a film's story out of its plot. The plot of *Some Like It Hot* covers a couple of weeks, but the story stretches back to include information about Sugar's former love life. The actual duration of the film – the screen duration – is one hour and fifty-five minutes. Typical ways of signalling time within a film include clocks, calendars and dialogue references.

Space is an important factor in narrative film. Stories need to take place somewhere. The action can take place in the city, in the country, in a hotel, in a character's house. Baz Luhrmann's *Romeo and Juliet* (1996), transposes the action of Shakespeare's well-known play from Verona, Italy, to Verona Beach in Los Angeles. In *Some Like It Hot*, places have particular importance; for example the jet-set, playboy setting of Miami is crucial to Sugar being able to meet the rich man of her dreams, and to Joe pulling off his impression of the heir to the Shell Oil fortune.

characters

A narrative, most importantly, also has characters. The most fully developed characters are usually the main protagonists and the chief point of identification for the audience. Characters and their traits, particularly desire, are usually at the root of cause and effect in a film. Characters may be developed, underdeveloped, major or minor; each will have a different relationship to cause and effect in the film. Generally speaking it is the main, most developed characters that drive the narrative forward through their actions: Joe impersonates a millionaire to get Sugar to fall for him.

a question of life and death

However, minor characters can have quite an important effect, such as when Nellie tells Joe and Jerry that Poliakoff is looking for two musicians: 'Well, it just so happens that he is looking for a bass and a sax.' Similarly a significant character will usually have more developed and recognisable character traits than a smaller character. Thus Sugar has more notable traits than Sweet Sue. Character traits can include anything from tastes and preferences to attitudes, qualities, dress, appearance and speech. The principal causal agents of any film are the characters. As Billy Wilder explains:

> If the gangsters who are chasing them see them as women, only as women, then ... once they are seen as men, they are *dead*. It's life and death. They cannot come out into the open. It's a question of life and death. That triggered everything. So we began to have a picture.
>
> *Crowe, 1999*

Characters have a different function at different times during a film. During the exposition, characters will reveal their current states of mind; in Joe and Jerry's case they need money to pay off everyone they have borrowed from, they need food and Jerry needs to see a dentist, much to Joe's disdain, 'We been out of work for four months – and you want to blow your first week's pay on your teeth?' Towards the middle of the film the characters will work towards achieving their goals, so Joe impersonates a millionaire in order to win Sugar, until by the end they have achieved their goals and everything has been resolved.

SUGAR KANE

Sugar is a neurotic, vulnerable, naïve young woman. She's also a funny, sexy, sassy lady, well aware of her physical proportions, and making the most of her assets with the clothes she wears. Sugar has always had bad luck with men, but this doesn't stop her hoping that she is going to meet Mr Right. She wants to find a husband – for preference, a millionaire. She can even describe the type of man she is looking for: 'I want mine to wear glasses, men who wear glasses are so much more gentle and sweet and helpless.'

tired of getting the fuzzy end of the lollipop

Although the way she's treated suggests Sugar is the black sheep of the band, her background is actually steeped in music. Her mother taught the piano, and her father was a conductor. She doesn't much rate her own abilities though, saying, 'I play the ukulele and I sing too ... I don't really have much of a voice but then it's not much of a band.' One of Sugar's most endearing qualities is precisely this awareness of her own shortcomings. She knows her weakness for men – especially saxophone players:

You fall for them and you really love 'em ... and the next thing you know, they're borrowing money from you and spending it on other dames and betting on horses.

It is Sugar's misfortune, then, to be working in an all-girl band for Sweet Sue, who forbids her girls from fraternising with men. At heart she's a good-time girl, looking for fun whilst meaning well. Her ideal man she describes as 'gentle and sweet'. She can sing 'I'm Through With Love' with soul, suggesting profound experience of heartbreak.

Sugar's other Achilles heel is drink. Alcohol numbs her unhappiness. She befriends Josephine and Daphne when they cover up for her as a concealed bottle slips from her garter. World-weary, she describes getting caught drinking as, 'the story of my life'.

But this very self-awareness wins her our hearts, not to mention Joe's (as she confides in him dressed as Josephine). Sugar is well acquainted with bad fortune, but declares, 'It's not going to happen to me again. Ever. I'm tired of getting the fuzzy end of the lollipop.' This determination in the face of a cruel Lady Luck endears Sugar to us all the more.

We should not forget though that Sugar is far from helpless. She knows her weaknesses, but she also knows her strengths. Her dress sense highlights her hourglass proportions and she seduces Junior on his yacht with a steady confidence in her own kissing abilities. When we first meet Sugar (through Joe and Jerry) she mysteriously claims to be 'running away'. Whilst this may suggest she's been dealt a poor hand in life, Sugar's inner strengths are considerable and they enable her to end *Some Like It Hot* on a note full of hope for a happy future.

a womaniser and a gambler

JOE (AKA JOSEPHINE: AKA JUNIOR)

In the course of *Some Like It Hot*, Joe switches to Josephine then to Junior, and back again so much that even he gets confused. Billy Wilder, with a playful love of character names, has all three begin with J. Needless to say, Joe is the character to whom everything happens, whatever disguise he's in. When we first encounter him, he's on stage at a speakeasy, playing saxophone in a band with Jerry, eyeing up a shapely tap-dancer. From the off, Joe is a womaniser and a gambler, planning to bet all his wages – and Jerry's – on a dog called Greased Lightning. When Jerry voices his doubts, Joe retorts with, 'Why do you have to paint everything so black? Suppose you get hit by a truck? Suppose the stock market crashes?' Joe's lack of foresight is comical. The dog doesn't win, and in 1929 the stock market did crash – and how (see Contexts). Joe is hedonistic, living for today and hoping for the best. Portrayed this way, Joe is set up as the ideal partner for Sugar Kane (who we've yet to meet). She's the good-time girl to his good-time man. Ironically, Joe disguises himself twice before revealing his true nature to Sugar.

When Jerry suggests they pose as women and head for Florida, Joe tells him to 'knock it off'. Even so, when needs must, it is Joe that makes the call to Poliakoff, and when they transform themselves into Josephine and Daphne, it is Josephine who makes the more convincing woman. Joe's restraint works in his favour. Jerry's Daphne is a flamboyant and talkative woman. Josephine is quieter and more reflective. In moments when they're alone, it is Joe that tells Jerry to 'Just keep telling yourself you're a girl,' as Jerry intones, 'I'm a girl, I'm a girl, I'm a girl.' Bizarrely, Joe and Jerry are like a married couple – Jerry even confesses to Osgood, that he's been living with a saxophone player for three years. It is clear, though, that Joe wears the trousers in this relationship – even when he's wearing a dress.

As Josephine, Joe goes on a journey that sets his perspective on gender straight. His previous relationships with women have been fraught. Early on, we see him seduce Poliakoff's secretary Nellie, only to manipulate her into lending him her car, leaving her disappointed. In playing a woman though, Joe sees life from the other side. When he arrives at the hotel, a bellboy tries to chat him up. Meeting up with Jerry, who has just encountered the attentions of Osgood Fielding III, Joe bemoans, 'Now you know how the other half lives ... they don't care – just as long as you wear skirts.' Joe never really rejects his shallow ways, but his time as a woman broadens his experience and readies him for properly relating to one – namely Sugar.

Joe as Josephine is wily enough to use his frustrating role as Sugar's confidante ultimately to his advantage. On the train to Miami, Sugar discusses her specifications for the millionaire that she dreams of meeting, 'I don't care how rich he is – as long as he has a yacht ... [and] I want mine to wear glasses.' Sure enough, on arriving in Miami, Sugar meets Junior (Joe in a precisely designed disguise) on the beach. (Like Josephine, the voice and mannerisms of Junior stem from an actor popular at the time of the film: this time the suave and sophisticated Cary Grant. In fact, Cary Grant was one of the biggest box-office draws in 1958/9 – see Contexts). Sugar is duly enchanted by Junior but Junior isn't actually as sophisticated a persona as Josephine. Joe has some understanding of women, but none of filthy-rich sons of oil magnates. Junior remains a one-dimensional disguise, prone to referring languidly to cocktails, motor boats and champagne. His one master stroke is to act emotionally damaged when alone with Sugar on Osgood's boat – with the result that Sugar tries all the harder to arouse his passion. This, however, is Joe's manipulation of women shining through. Junior also gets the line, 'Well, I guess some like it hot,' referring to Sugar's part in a 'red hot' jazz band – although he adds, 'personally I prefer classical music.'

All along, Junior is a mask for Joe to wear which he thinks will attract Sugar. Eventually, when Joe ceases to manipulate Sugar and simply acts as himself, Sugar is delighted and stays unquestioningly by his side. She really wasn't suited to Junior anyway. Speaking to Sugar as Joe for the first time, he says, 'You don't want me, Sugar, I'm a liar and a phoney. A saxophone player – one of those no-goodniks you've been running away from.' But Sugar is undeterred. They have both met their match.

JERRY (AKA DAPHNE)

Jerry, as Daphne, lends himself less well to role-playing than Joe masquerading as Josephine. His character hardly alters at all and, unlike Joe, he never gets to attempt a third persona.

jittery Jerry becomes jittery Daphne

When we meet Jerry, playing bass in the speakeasy band, he's already displaying the traits we come to recognise him by. He fancifully suggests spending his next wage packet at the dentist's, 'I lost a filling in my back teeth, It's just a little inlay – it doesn't have to be gold.'

It takes the more pragmatic Joe to point out that they are up to their ears in debt. But when Jerry agrees that they should pay everybody a 'little something on account', Joe puts forward an alternative – betting the lot on a dog. Joe gets his way, and they lose the money.

Throughout *Some Like It Hot*, Jerry's ideas seem to come direct from cloud-cuckoo-land, but when put into practice they work, and his wild imagination often wins out over Joe's pragmatic approach. Jerry's idea of impersonating women to escape Chicago and get the job in Miami seems outlandish, and at first Joe refuses even to consider it. Ultimately, though, they go through with it and it saves their skin.

Jerry's freewheeling, nervous energy often gets the pair into hot water. When they encounter the gangsters at Charlie's Garage, it is Jerry that can't keep from talking while they hide. Joe has to cover his mouth. On being discovered, Jerry is 'quavering', and tries to excuse them, 'It's none of our business if you guys want to knock each other off,' at which Joe nudges him violently. It's not surprising then, that jittery Jerry becomes jittery Daphne. Jerry might be said to have a feminine side already. He's imaginative, not very practical and prone to meekness and nervousness. Certainly this is how audiences of 1959 would be used to seeing women represented, and Jerry has markedly more femininity than Joe. So while Joe makes a believable Josephine by use of his natural self-restraint, Jerry as Daphne puts in less effort, but pulls off the role through displaying his naturally feminine side.

On boarding the train for Miami, Joe is surprised to find that Jerry has changed his female name from Geraldine – 'I never did like the name Geraldine' – to the ultra-feminine 'Daphne', and in doing so moves another step away from his masculine self. Even the link to his own name is gone. Clearly Joe, as Josephine, is carefully playing a part, but Jerry as Daphne is indulging something within himself, with considerably less care. Indeed, who's the lucky girl?

when lusty thoughts overcome Jerry, it is Josephine that scolds him and points him back to the mantra, 'I'm a girl.'

It takes all of Jerry's will-power to resist the curvy charms of Sugar, especially when she climbs into his bunk for a 'girly' chat and a drink after lights-out. (In a scene present in the screenplay but excised during filming, Jerry later confesses his secret to Sugar in a darkened bunk – 'there are all sorts of things about me that are not natural – I'm a boy.' Unfortunately Jerry has slipped into the wrong bunk and confessed this to an enraged Joe. However, Billy Wilder decided the scene wasn't necessary.) In Miami, Jerry is so successfully feminine that Daphne gets her own millionaire admirer – albeit an elderly one – in the form of Osgood Fielding III. For Joe, posing as a woman is a useful nuisance. But Jerry comes to relish the experience and the attentions of Osgood. At first the courtship is an irritant, and Jerry is cagey, but he continues to flirt with Osgood, even if subconsciously, 'You know something Mr Fielding? You're dynamite!' Jerry quite forgets himself when he makes the following announcement to Joe:

```
Jerry (beaming)
      I'm engaged.
Joe
      Congratulations, who's the lucky girl?
Jerry
      I am.
```

Jerry's plan to tell Osgood the truth 'when the time comes', causes Joe to explode: 'There are laws, conventions – it's just not being done.' Joe even has to give Jerry a new mantra to reluctantly intone: 'I'm a boy ... I'm a boy ...' To Joe, becoming a woman requires care and effort. Jerry does it simply by forgetting he's a man.

Joe's romance with Sugar is the meat of the film, and Jerry's liaison with Osgood is pure comedy to throw the former into relief. Consider the way Joe's first kiss with Sugar is intercut with Osgood and Jerry's tango to magnificent comic effect. Of course, the conclusion of the film famously lies with Jerry, publicly casting off his female persona long after Josephine is revealed as Joe. Indeed, the final lines are amongst the most successful and famed in all of screen comedy – fittingly, as comedy is the main business of *Some Like It Hot*. But as regards Jerry, what are we to assume from this conclusion? He masquerades as a woman so successfully that he finds himself a male partner, and submerges his masculinity so fully that he only resurfaces as Jerry in the closing seconds out of desperation. In the screenplay, the final stage direction asks: 'how is he going to get himself out of this?' All comic intent aside, Jerry's gender confusion has become absolute.

OSGOOD FIELDING III

Despite the fact that he has been married so many times that he has lost count – 'Mama is keeping score' – Osgood thinks he's looking at the new Mrs Fielding III when he sees Daphne, proposing after just one night out together. He's a mummy's boy, but with an eye for the ladies. He likes to have a good time and knows how to party. When he and Daphne go on their date, Osgood suggests that they 'blindfold the orchestra and tango till dawn'. He is generous with his money and sets about wooing Daphne, showering her with flowers and expensive gifts. Undeterred by the number of ex-wives he has, he is keen to make an honest woman of her – even when he discovers that she is really a he – giving rise to the last line of the film, 'Well, nobody's perfect'.

If Junior is a photofit ideal of the sort of millionaire Sweet Sue's girls dream of meeting, then Osgood is the less ideal reality. In fact, his personality is a great deal more appealing than Junior's. Osgood is basically a good man, generous and patient in his pursuit of Daphne. His slight lasciviousness aside, he has an appealing sense of fun which even leads Jerry to forget himself and enjoy their time together. Osgood might be somewhat simple – forgetting his total of ex-wives, and dismissing Daphne's every excuse not to marry, up to and including 'I'm a boy' – but equally this is evidence of a happy-go-lucky soul without a streak of bitterness or cunning. Indeed, the thought of Osgood actively seeking an ideal wife, no matter how many times he's got it wrong, makes him likeably optimistic, and perhaps even the only character in *Some Like It Hot* who is complete and at ease when we meet him, and unchanged come the end.

a dangerous man to know

SPATS COLOMBO

So-called because of his distinctive trademark – his then-fashionable shoe gaiter. Spats Colombo is a dangerous man to know. He owns the speakeasy and he's always up to no good. Whether it's arranging for the next stash of booze to make its way into the city or finishing off the witnesses to one of his shoot-outs, he's not a man who knows the meaning of the word 'mercy'.

Basically a caricature of an Italian gangster boss – speaking out of the side of his mouth, in an Italian-American brogue and wearing all the latest fashions – Spats has no depth at all. His function in the film is to provide Joe and Jerry with an **antagonist** to escape from. Billy Wilder wants us to recognise what Spats is, with a minimum of fuss: he even cast George Raft, well-known for his gangster roles (see Contexts: Genre) to make the point abundantly clear.

Gangster bosses are traditionally humourless souls, and as a gangster cipher Spats isn't suited to comic lines. But writers Billy Wilder and I.A.L. Diamond are in the business of comedy, famed for their funny dialogue and for characters that suit saying it. So Spats never rises above the status of cardboard cut-out. He can't get a laugh, so the writers keep his screen time to a minimum and concentrate on characters who can.

SWEET SUE

Like Spats, Sweet Sue never really moves beyond being a cipher, and she doesn't have many lines. While not as humour-free as Spats, she's still a stern character from which the antics of the girls in the band must be hidden. As such Sue is another functional nemesis. For Sugar, Sue is her exact opposite number, who struggles to prevent the band access to either men or liquor – Sugar's twin weaknesses. So Sugar must constantly take private swigs from her hidden hip flask. Joe and Jerry, too, have their own secrets to conceal from Sue.

Sue is a figure to be avoided. She scolds her girls for every misdemeanour, and most often her role in a scene is to react to the actions of others – usually with shock. Occasionally her actions as a 'straight man' cause laughs, but generally the fun is elsewhere. Billy Wilder and I.A.L. Diamond know this, and keep Sue's presence to the absolute minimum.

narrator/author

When a character recounts story actions or information that we don't actually see within the diegesis, they are narrating the film. We see them as a narrator or the source of narration. Narration can be restricted or unrestricted. A usual way of approaching narration is to ask, 'who knows what and when?' Different characters are privileged with different information at any one time. Jerry knows that Joe is dressing up and impersonating a millionaire, yet nobody, not even the audience, knows that the mob are going to turn up at the hotel. Nothing has prepared us for this, and in fact we have been led away from the mob storyline, since we are now fully involved with the romance taking place between Joe and Sugar.

themes

The main themes of *Some Like It Hot* are premarital sex, role-playing and forbidden pleasure.

PREMARITAL SEX

It is clear from the original publicity campaign – the poster and the trailer – that sex is a selling point of the film. The poster shows Marilyn Monroe, on the shoulders of Tony Curtis and Jack Lemmon, wearing a flimsy, low-cut dress, with the tag line, 'Marilyn Monroe and her bosom companions', whilst the trailer goes through all the elements of the film until it says, 'You've never laughed more at sex or a picture about it' (see Contexts: Marketing). Sex was possibly even more of a selling point then than it is today. With censorship still extremely strict, sex in the movies was a little known, illicit proposition. Billy Wilder used the burgeoning new morality as an opportunity to make a film that was unusually upfront in its attitudes to sex. The film is full of references to sex. Sweet Sue makes it known very early on, when Josephine and Daphne join the band, that she prohibits two things, 'liquor and men'. Daphne readily explains that this won't be a problem, 'Men, we wouldn't be caught dead with them. Rough, hairy beasts. Eight hands. And they all just want one thing from a girl.' Later on when everyone is getting undressed and ready for bed, Joe has to tell Jerry to keep his desires in check,

Joe

Steady boy. Just keep telling yourself you're a girl.

Jerry

I'm a girl. I'm a girl. I'm a girl.

When the band arrive at the Seminole Ritz hotel in Florida, as the girls had hoped, millionaires are lined up to greet them. Oil magnate, Osgood Fielding III exclaims his trademark 'zowie' making no bones about the fact that he is definitely interested in Daphne and her physical attributes:

Osgood

I'm Osgood Fielding III.

Daphne

I'm Cinderella the second.

Osgood

If it's one thing I admire, it's a girl with a shapely ankle.

Sugar is open about her past, clearing indicating that she has had sexual relationships with men before, at a time when 'nice girls don't' would still have been the dominant attitude towards sex before marriage. When it comes to being alone on the boat with Junior, she doesn't seem at all nervous or worried at being without a chaperone so late at night, alone with a man; this is borne out by the way in which she delivers the line, 'You know, I've never been completely alone with a man before – in the middle of the night – in the middle of the ocean.' Ironically, she ends up seducing him, when he plays the 'impotence card'. She certainly doesn't seem ill at ease and is more than eager to help him get over his problem, asking him, 'Have you ever tried American girls?' Billy Wilder has talked at length about this scene, and how it was significant that they subverted

Daphne meets Osgood

'If there's one thing I admire
it's a girl with a shapely ankle'

the traditional boy seduces girl scene. It may not have worked so well if an actress less well known for her sexual charms had been playing the role.

Sweet Sue makes a subtle reference to the sexual status of the girls in the band when she describes them as 'virtuosos', an unlikelyhood given the crude innuendo and dirty jokes we've heard the girls telling earlier. Attitudes towards sex come out at other times, such as the fact that Osgood wants to marry Daphne straight away, suggesting that he doesn't go in for sex before marriage.

ROLE-PLAYING

The last message we take from *Some Like It Hot* is simply 'nobody's perfect'. But if nobody in the world of the film is perfect, then it follows that everyone is striving to overcome their shortcomings.

In fact, everyone in *Some Like It Hot* can be said to be playing a role of some sort. The majority of characters are actually musicians, and therefore public performers. Jerry and Joe absolutely must masquerade as women – out of sheer necessity – but later Joe creates another persona; Osgood plays the part of the lecherous old man; the bellboy plays the part of a chancer, undeterred by Josephine's lack of interest in him; Sugar plays on the dumb blonde **stereotype** to explain away the fact that she continues to make the same mistakes with men, 'I'm not very bright.'

The role-playing, and the disguises that go with it, whether literally dressing up as someone else, or simply exploiting the character's traits to the maximum, gives the film a knockabout farce quality, a pantomime effect in which men chase other men, dressed as women, through a hotel lobby. This role-playing adds to the 'staginess' of the film and allows other characters to ham it up – the gangsters are mean and vicious, the girls in the band are ditzy, and the bellboy relishes playing the lecherous young male. At the same time, Jerry seems to quite forget who he is at times, taking his enjoyment of playing a female character so far that he gets engaged to a man. It is interesting then that *Some Like It Hot* ultimately disapproves of role-playing. Most of the characters in the film don't respond as people but as types – the dumb blonde, the spoilt millionaire ...

subtle condemnation of role-playing

To win Sugar, Joe must not only pretend that he is the heir to a multinational company, but also act out a Hollywood stereotype of the smooth, suave and sophisticated variety (albeit with a comic touch) by adopting a Cary-Grant-style accent. In the final scenes, though, he reveals his true self, and only then can Sugar fully love him. This need for all masks finally to be removed highlights the film's subtle condemnation of role-playing.

FORBIDDEN PLEASURE

As the title suggests, some like it hot. From the opening scene we are aware that the setting is during America's Prohibition and alcohol is illegal. Spats's gang are going to great lengths to make alcohol available to those who want it. Throughout the film, characters are seen taking swigs from bottles and flasks. This appetite for pleasure is satisfied even though it's forbidden. Maybe it becomes even more pleasurable, precisely because of Prohibition. All the characters crave liquor, and it's never far from anyone's mind. When Sugar excitedly announces she has 'great news', Joe replies, 'What, they've repealed Prohibition?'

Alcohol isn't the only thing that's not allowed. Sweet Sue, the band leader, forbids Sugar's other vice: men. That doesn't stop Sugar from trying though, and in the course of the film Sugar has many a drink and she finds herself a man. Initially she doesn't know she has – precisely because Josephine is indulging in another taboo – cross-dressing. It's done out of life or death necessity, although Joe balks at the idea initially – as he says to Jerry, 'You've flipped your wig.'

In due course, though, the escapade has its plusses, and the guys become quite comfortable dressed as women. Daphne comes to relish being wooed by Osgood, getting quite carried away with it all until Joe confronts Jerry with reality:

```
Joe
      What are you going to do on your honeymoon?
Jerry
      He wants to go to the Riviera, but I kinda
      lean towards Niagara Falls.
```

Although chiefly for comic effect, this tack is subversive and transgressive. The famous conclusion – 'Well, nobody's perfect' – is never explored, although Billy Wilder and I.A.L. Diamond mischievously hint at it in the note that closes the screenplay. 'How is (Jerry) going to get himself out of this? But that's another story – and we're not quite sure the public is ready for it.' Homosexuality is never tackled head-on, but in 1920s America it would have been very much a taboo – a forbidden pleasure in itself. As indeed it would still be in 1959, a period of transition, when post-war conservatism had yet to give way to the freer thinking, sexually liberated 1960s. Note too that although the relationship between Jerry and Osgood is a sound source of comedy, when Joe flees the gangsters, he forgets himself and kisses Sugar whilst still in full Josephine get-up: Sweet Sue's reaction to the sight of two women kissing is to appear very shocked. The comic potential of lesbianism is territory the film can't explore.

The theme of forbidden pleasure would be as apt for the period in which the film was seen as it was for the age in which it was set.

parallelism

Parallelism is the process in which 'the film cues the spectator to compare two or more distinct elements by highlighting some similarity' (Bordwell and Thompson, 1993). Sugar wants to meet a millionaire whilst a millionaire falls for Daphne. Sugar always falls for the no-good saxophone players, only to be left with, 'a pair of old socks and a tube of toothpaste, all squeezed out' after they have gone. Unwittingly, by falling for Junior she is actually falling for the same type again. Joe has a track record of treating women just as badly as men have treated Sugar, as suggested to us when we learn that he has stood Nellie up and borrowed money from all the girls in the band.

Other examples of parallelism revolve around motifs in the film. Drink is a key motif: it is Prohibition and drinking is illegal. The film starts with a close-up shot of a casket being opened to reveal a stash of booze. The illegal drinking party is raided by the police. We learn early on that Sugar likes to drink to drown her sorrows; when the girls throw a party on the train, they drink alcohol out of a hot-water bottle; Sweet Sue won't tolerate liquor, and when Sugar rushes up to Josephine to tell her something wonderful has happened, she replies with, 'What, they've repealed Prohibition?' (see Themes).

opening/closure

A defining feature of classical Hollywood cinema is closure. Everything is tied up neatly at the end of the film and the audience has a strong sense of the outcome of most major events and the fate of the main characters. In mainstream films, closure is usually a logical conclusion to events. Towards the end of *Some Like It Hot* the gangsters turn up at the hotel – at a point when the audience has pretty much forgotten all about them. The gangsters' presence reminds us why Joe and Jerry are dressed up as women, which in turn reminds us of the characters' original goals. Joe dashes to Sugar, dressed as Josephine, almost forgetting himself, as she is on the bandstand singing the poignant, 'I'm Through With Love'. When one of the gangsters shouts out, 'That's no dame', Sugar suddenly clicks. Joe and Jerry are chased by the gangsters out of the hotel, to the harbour, where Osgood is waiting. Sugar realises that Junior is Josephine – who is really a man, one of those, 'no-goodniks' she's been running away from – and immediately chases after them, shouting: 'Wait for me – Sugar!'

Film theorist David Bordwell states that out of a random sample of over a hundred Hollywood films, sixty ended with the cliché happy ending, the romantic clinch. *Some Like It Hot* almost ends like this, on a shot of Joe and Sugar kissing in the back of the boat, but instead, the last lines of dialogue go to Daphne and Osgood, as Daphne tries to explain to Osgood that they can never be together, saying, 'Look, Osgood – I'm going to level with you. We can't get married at all'. Osgood is undeterred by Daphne's protests that she can't wear his mother's wedding dress, she smokes and that she can never have children, until finally, ripping off the wig, 'Daphne' declares: 'I'm a man'. To which Osgood replies with the final line of the film, 'Well, nobody's perfect'.

If we compare the end of *Some Like It Hot* with the beginning we have moved from cold, dreary, dismal Chicago, where crime is rife and times are hard, to warm, inviting Florida, where millionaires are ten a penny and the sun always shines. Events have turned full circle, in that the gangsters have turned up unexpectedly, with the only differences being that they have changed out of their dark, sombre threatening clothes into something lighter and more summery. Some of the issues important at the beginning of the film, such as Joe and Jerry's search for work, don't seem to be quite so significant, and at any rate, Jerry has found himself a millionaire husband. Joe on the other hand seems to have exchanged his Jack the Lad quality for the love of Sugar, or is this just a phase, blinded by her beauty, only to return to his old ways, when the love turns sour? This we'll never know.

style

As well as being a story, a film is a combination of different cinematic elements. These include mise-en-scène, cinematography, editing and sound; they combine together to make a scene work and constitute a film's style. For instance: when Sugar steps on to the motor boat in which Joe (disguised as Junior) is waiting, figure movement and setting are provided as mise-en-scène; it is past midnight so the sky is dark (provided as lighting). Sugar is the object of the camera (cinematography); we can hear both the purr of the engine starting (sound) and the conversation between Sugar and Joe (sound).

The elements that have gone into making this scene work have been thoroughly thought through. Many of them would have been considered during the scriptwriting process and will exist as direction in the screenplay. Some will have been brainstormed on set with the art director, cinematographer and sound engineer. Style thus helps the viewer to construct a coherent and consistent time and space in which the film's action occurs: for example, lighting will help define figures; colour will highlight planes; the main character will be positioned in the centre of the frame; and maximum clarity of dialogue will be ensured. It is essential that everything is clear at the level of denotation.

mise-en-scène

Mise-en-scène was originally a theatre term. It approximately translates as 'what's in the scene', and it is the director's control over what ends up in the frame. Mise-en-scène includes the set, lighting, costume plus figure movement and behaviour. The mise-en-scène is important in that it can create visual continuity:

> Many motifs that recur in the course of the plot's unfolding are visual elements of the mise-en-scène, and such motifs can

settings, objects and characters all have narrative functions

> contribute significantly to the fundamental formal principles of the film's overall organisation: its unity and its patterns of similarity, difference, and development.
>
> *Bordwell and Thompson, 1993*

Certain aspects of the mise-en-scène can also be responsible for moving the narrative forward. Settings, objects and characters all have narrative functions. Specific settings fulfil distinct narrative functions: for instance, it's cold in Chicago, emphasising the need for Joe and Jerry to get work after they have hocked their coats. The same motivation of narrative applies to the film's use of costume. Josephine and Daphne are significantly different from the girls in the band, with their high-necked, long flannel nightgowns contrasting with the short, sexy night attire of the other 'real' women. Aspects of a film's mise-en-scène, such as costume or lighting, are often what we remember after seeing a film. The opening sequence of *Some Like It Hot* is particularly memorable due to the striking use of such elements. The film opens on a dark, windy Chicago evening. Police sirens are sounding and a hearse is making its way through the city centre at breakneck speed. Local mobsters are seen escaping a police shoot-out, and we cut to a close-up camera shot of the lid of a casket being lifted to reveal a stash of alcohol. The words 'Chicago 1929' come up on screen, superimposed over the shot.

The mise-en-scène can also have a symbolic function, highlighting contrasts in a film. The scene of the party in Daphne's bunk ends with Daphne pulling the emergency cord and Bienstock sleepily emerging from his bunk asking 'Are we in Florida?' This brings a comic conclusion to the first part of the film, gently ushering the audience into the next part, which will open on a set and setting that is in marked contrast to the harsh social environment of Chicago. Bienstock's query is followed by a dissolve, and the next shot is an obvious signifier of sunnier climes – palm trees. Immediately a complete contrast is set up to the unfriendly place we've left behind. The scene proper begins with an establishing shot of a sumptuous hotel, where the next lot of action will be played out; we cut to a host of rich old men, sitting lined up, smiling and ready to make the girls' acquaintance. We are clearly now in a very different place altogether. The

You can't trust those guys

Contrast between the girls' nightwear

opulent architecture of the art deco buildings and hotels frames the landscape and you can almost smell and taste the grandeur of the place.

set design and setting

The set design takes the style of the late 1920s and filters it through the more modern aesthetic of the late 1950s when the film was made. Each set is pertinent to the connotative function of the scene. The elegant hotel makes an appropriate place for millionaires to be holed up during the cold winter months. The Chicago scenes reveal a series of 1920s-style exteriors and interiors, including narrow streets, tall buildings and the ornate, gilt mirrors in the speakeasy. The two settings in which the film takes place – Chicago and Miami – are polar opposites in character. Grim, dark Chicago is populated by vicious hoods eager to get their hands on every dollar that's up for grabs, whilst on the other hand sunny Miami has a positive air and is full of millionaires keen to put their riches the way of any suitable attractive females (see Style: Lighting). It is easy to.tell the difference between the scenes in Chicago, which were shot on a studio back-lot, lending them a claustrophobic atmosphere and the outdoors Miami scenes, which were all shot on location. The location setting provides the brighter, breezier tone necessary for this part of the film.

costume

The costumes in *Some Like It Hot* mostly attempt to be authentic to the milieu in which the film is set. According to the screenplay, the dancers at the speakeasy wear 'racoon coats and beanies', whilst the band wear 'threadbare tuxedos', emphasising their economic hardship. In actual fact the dancers aren't quite dressed like this in the finished film, but they are clearly wearing outfits reminiscent of the period. When we first see Joe and Jerry as 'Josephine' and 'Daphne', their attire is described as follows, 'rolled up stockings, short dresses, coats with cheap fur pieces, and rakish cloche hats'.

Adding to the period look, their make-up was a combination of the heavy eyelashes and smudged eyeshadow of the 1920s, although thick 1950s

revealing, tight, glamorous, undeniably 1950s outfits

eyebrows and full lips are also in evidence suggesting that however much *Some Like It Hot* was at pains to capture the look of the 1920s, it inevitably falls victim to a 1950s style at times. No matter how much a costume designer or production designer attempts to recreate a look from another period, the style and influence of the period in which something is made will often have an unconscious effect on the overall look.

Fortunately for Joe and Jerry, whose female attributes aren't exactly their best features, the straight-up-and-down look was all the rage in the 1920s. But the flat-chested style, so de rigueur at this time, was inappropriate for Marilyn Monroe. With her ample womanly proportions, there would have been little point in trying to flatten her chest into a period-style dress. Instead she wears a series of revealing, tight, glamorous, undeniably 1950s outfits and gowns, which is partly what the audience would have paid their money to see. For the film's second song, Sugar sings 'I Wanna Be Loved By You', wearing a flesh-coloured, virtually transparent dress which gives her the appearance of being bare-breasted (risqué in 1959, and quite unthinkable in 1929 when the film is set). When the film was first released it was given an 'A' certificate (equivalent to today's PG, although as a sign of changing attitudes the 1989 video release was awarded a U certificate). With a dress of sequinned material and a low-cut back, Marilyn Monroe as Sugar looks every inch the Hollywood film star that the audience would have expected.

In contrast, Josephine and Daphne sport flapper-style dresses appropriate to the period. Even on arrival in Florida, when Sugar wears a white, clinging, modern outfit, the pair still favour the safety of the high-neck look. In this sense, it's arguable that Marilyn Monroe's star presence disrupts the narrative flow (see Narrative & form: Narrative).

Other notable costumes in the film are those of the gangsters. Spats Colombo wears typical gangster attire – smart suits, trilbys and his trademark spats. When Spats arrives at the garage there is an identifying close-up, shot feet first. Costume and clothes can even contribute to a film's narrative: Joe steals Bienstock's glasses and suitcase full of clothes, as he has in mind to dress up as a millionaire, fulfilling Sugar's description of how she wants her ideal man to look: 'I want mine to wear glasses.'

Sugar in revealing attire

lighting

The impact of an image often comes from the way in which it is lit. In cinema, lighting illuminates the scene, enabling the viewer to see the action – but it also has an effect on mood, setting, tone and texture. Lighter and darker areas within the frame contribute to the overall composition of each shot, guiding our attention to significant objects and actions.

Lighting can also be used symbolically, either to lighten or to darken the tone of individual scenes. In *Some Like It Hot*, this is most notable in the change of light between Chicago and Florida. The gangster-infested scenes in Chicago are shot using very low non-naturalistic studio lights: these darkly lit scenes have a sinister and threatening atmosphere. The Florida scenes later in the film are brightly lit, emphasising the different nature of this new setting. We are no longer in a place where crime is rife and everyone is unemployed: here the sun is shining, millionaires are everywhere and everyone is having fun. The dark, oppressive city is far away.

Lighting is even used suggestively in *Some Like It Hot*. As Sugar sings 'I Wanna Be Loved By You', her head and shoulders are spotlit: her chest is in shadow, but the cumulative effect – combined with the diaphanous areas of the dress she's wearing – make it appear that we can see her breasts through it. We can't – it is just the design of the dress – but it is lighting trickery which subliminally suggests more sexually alluring nudity than is shown on screen.

dialogue & performance

When it came to writing a screenplay, Billy Wilder and I.A.L. Diamond had a set routine. As Billy Wilder says:

> I'd sit at my desk, he'd slouch in the black chair, his feet on the ottoman, chewing gum ... sometimes the muses would come and kiss our brow and we'd whip up ten or twelve pages per day, Iz on the typewriter, me on the yellow pad. There was no arm twisting, pulling rank, shouting or screaming.
>
> *Cousins, 1988*

dialogue & performance

specific directorial instructions

Despite Billy Wilder's claims that he wrote minimal scripts, the *Some Like It Hot* screenplay – dated July 1958 – contains specific directorial instructions, with every dissolve and fade marked. The screenplay even carries detailed description of the settings, and often reveals the mischievous style of Billy Wilder and I.A.L. Diamond: in the mourning scene, as the sergeant enters the speakeasy, the direction reads, 'Grandma must have been quite a person, because she left a lot of condoling friends behind, and they are holding a very lively wake.'

There are noteworthy differences between the screenplay and the finished film. In the film, the scene on the train ends with Bienstock's line, 'Are we in Florida?' In the screenplay, however, the scene continues for four pages. Here Joe swaps berths with Sugar, so that she doesn't have to sleep over Bienstock, who snores heavily; and Jerry rehearses telling Sugar that he's not what he seems: 'What I'm trying to say is – my name isn't really Daphne – it's Geraldine – I mean, Jerry – and you know why it's Jerry? – because I'm a boy.' Joe is furious at Jerry's willingness to betray them both, and at his wish to seduce Sugar: 'I ought to slug you!' These additional pages of script were presumably cut because they are superfluous. They don't advance the action and add nothing to the narrative. They simply extend the joke of their changed identities, with the scene ending as Jerry says to Joe, 'You wouldn't hit a girl would you?'

There are several other minor changes between the screenplay and the film. Mainly, specific words are altered, such as in Sweet Sue's address to the audience after the band's first performance at the hotel. In the screenplay, she says, 'This is Sweet Sue, saying goodnight, and reminding all you wolves out there, every girl in my band is a virtuoso and I intend to keep it that way.' In the final film, the word 'wolves' is changed to 'daddies'. The change is more in keeping with the fact that the audience is made up chiefly of the ageing millionaires we saw earlier – whose days as sexual predators are effectively over.

Naturally, the screenplay comes to life through the performances of the actors. It is the way an actor interprets a role, including the gestures, facial expressions and voice they select for a role, that is significant. When the

Sugar is centre stage

band rehearse on the train, Sugar is clearly centre stage, both as the centrepiece of the band – she's the singer after all – and in terms of the hierarchy of the actors on screen, with the other band members all framing her. She sings 'Running Wild', and plays her ukulele as the camera cuts back and forth between close-ups and medium close-ups of her, and of Josephine and Daphne on sax and bass.

The camera obviously adores Marilyn Monroe and she responds accordingly. As she moves back and forth, swaying and swinging her hips provocatively, her full figure is once again highlighted by the tight-fitting dress she is wearing, and she plays up the role of the sexy showgirl for all she's worth. The camera shoots her from behind, focusing on her wiggling hips and gutsy performance.

Tony Curtis's millionaire persona, Junior, spoofs English upper-class types. His vocal impression would have been recognised by movie-goers in the late 1950s (although in 1929, the year in which the film is set, Cary Grant was yet to appear in a film). Jerry is particularly peeved by Joe's impression, not least because he had designs on Sugar too, saying, 'Nobody talks like that', imitating the clipped Cary Grant tones back to him.

sound

The sound design of the film appears not to have been a concern of Billy Wilder's. Indeed, his mastery of well-scripted dialogue ensures that hardly a moment goes by that isn't filled by finely crafted lines. The only sound effects are standard diegetic sounds: machine-gun fire, the busy noise-filled station with the sound of passengers milling about and the station announcer calling out details of arrivals and departures and the rattle over the tracks of a moving locomotive.

There is obviously a strong musical element in the film, as virtually every character is a musician. The score, by Adolph Deutsch, is effective and unobtrusive, capturing as it does the 1920s setting with high-octane jazz. Sharp brassy strings in the score act as a threatening theme whenever Spats's gangsters appear; when they arrive in Miami, this theme signals the renewed threat to Joe and Jerry.

sound

three musical numbers

The main impact of the sound in *Some Like It Hot* comes from the three musical numbers, played by Sweet Sue and Her Society Syncopators and sung by Sugar Kane. The numbers are 'Running Wild' (performed on the train en route to Miami), 'I Wanna Be Loved By You' (from the band's first performance at the hotel) and 'I'm Through With Love' (performed after Sugar has been informed by Junior that he's leaving for good). All three illustrate Sugar's feelings about love as she's performing: she's footloose and on the way to somewhere promising during 'Running Wild'; hoping to find love amongst the millionaires of Florida in 'I Wanna Be Loved By You' (Marilyn Monroe's performance here is one of the best-remembered scenes from her whole career); and heartbroken during 'I'm Through With Love'. In that respect, by communicating something to the audience that can't be shown on screen, the songs perform a similar function to another of Billy Wilder's favourite devices – the voice-over. It is also worth noting that the musical theme of 'Running Wild' recurs on Adolph Deutsch's score during several scenes, up until Sugar finds love with Junior.

The musical numbers of the film even inspired Jack Lemmon to record an album, released in 1959, featuring songs of the roaring twenties; thus giving the soundtrack life beyond the film.

cinematography

Cinematography is the photographic art of filming the image. Standard elements include duration and framing of a shot.

A common scene format might constitute an establishing shot, followed by a closer shot directing the viewer to the significant aspect of the scene/action, followed by further long shots to re-establish the setting, characters, faces, bodies and so on. Personality traits of characters, depicted through costume detail, facial expression etc., often require a close-up in order to accentuate them. If we take the example of the seduction scene, we can see how cinematography works, and how the camera is used to add resonance to the narrative.

At the very start of the scene the camera cuts between Joe cycling towards Osgood's motor boat and Sugar running along the harbour to meet Junior.

When Sugar gets into the boat, the camera shoots from the right at a high angle. The shot highlights her almost transparent dress, making it look as though her chest is bare. Once they are aboard Osgood's yacht, the seduction begins. As they kiss, the camera pans at tremendous speed to the left of the screen – and we see Daphne and Osgood dancing a tango on a crowded dance floor. The shot lasts just seconds before panning back quickly, this time to the right of the screen, until we see Junior and Sugar fully entwined. A top-speed pan acts as a cut: this camera effect enables us to follow both couples at once, and by panning across the screen rather than simply cutting, it emphasises that the seductions are taking place simultaneously.

black & white

By 1955 over fifty per cent of films being made were in colour. Billy Wilder was not a fan of making films in colour. He had made *The Seven Year Itch* in colour purely because Marilyn Monroe's contract demanded it. But since *Some Like It Hot* is set in 1929, it actually suits being shot in black and white, making it a more authentic representation of the period – or at least, how it would be known in cinema. The gangster films that a 1950s audience would have been familiar with would all have been made in black and white (see Contexts: Genre). Initially there was also the purely practical issue of how to shoot Jack Lemmon and Tony Curtis in full make-up, dressed as women, as convincingly as possible. Early tests in colour made them look unacceptably grotesque, but black and white photography – more pleasing to the eye, and less natural than colour – made the effect passable without looking too outlandish.

Billy Wilder's follow-up to *Some Like It Hot*, *The Apartment*, made in 1962, was also made in monochrome, yet this was no period piece: the film is set in contemporary America. This reinforces the fact that it was the pure aesthetic of black and white photography that appealed to Billy Wilder. Nevertheless, the use of black and white in *Some Like It Hot* is chiefly a functional choice, re-creating the 1920s period look. Although Marilyn Monroe's own preference was to be shot in colour, the black and white photography in *Some Like It Hot* produced some of the most enduring and

a technical necessity rather than a creative process

iconic images she is still remembered by, and as such the director's choice worked decidedly to her advantage.

The use of monochrome film even ties in with a concern at the heart of *Some Like It Hot*. Just as the differences between the sexes are a central **motif** in the film, so too the lack of colours in the image – just two, black and white, are shown – accentuates the polar nature of gender; perhaps even hinting at the possibilities of gender blending in its 'greyness'.

editing

Editing is one of the most frequently discussed aspects of film-making. A feature-length Hollywood film contains an average of between 800 and 1200 shots. In the editing process, an editor works with the director to juxtapose some shots and discard others. Different types of shots can be joined, and effects can be added during the editing process, such as a fade-out: the gradual darkening of an image to black; and a fade-in: from black to light.

Billy Wilder typically ends his shots with dissolves, briefly superimposing the end of one shot with the beginning of the next; and **wipes**, replacing one shot gradually with another. In cinema, the most common type of edit is a simple cut: Billy Wilder didn't favour cuts. He intentionally wrote his films so as not to require a long editing process. As a director, he saw editing as a technical necessity rather than a creative process.

Doane Harrison was Billy Wilder's long-term editor who had worked with him since his first American film. He was his right-hand man when it came to coordinating shots. By the time of *Some Like It Hot*, Doane Harrison has an associate **producer** credit. Billy Wilder still saw himself more as a writer than a director, and tended to rely on Doane Harrison's sense of which shots worked well together. In the continuity style of editing – the style most typical of mainstream cinema – the action is shot along a centre line, known as the 180-degree line. The idea is that the camera can be positioned at any point along this line, so long as it remains on one side of it, ensuring that portions of space are continuous from shot to shot.

'How do they walk in these things?'

The cinematography and the editing are important functions of the film and can help to further the narrative quickly and effectively. They are used with precision and skill at the crucial point where Joe and Jerry are escaping Spats's gang: disappearing into a drugstore to escape the mob and the police sirens, Joe asks Jerry for some money for the phone. Jerry is initially bemused that Joe wants to make a phone call at a time like this, until he hears Joe speak, and then he understands: 'Mr Poliakoff, I hear you're looking for a couple of girl musicians.'

The scene ends on a dissolve. The first shot of the next scene is a close-up of two pairs of stocking-clad legs. The camera stays on the legs from behind as they hobble, with great difficulty, along the platform. We cut to a front view, and discover that the bandy legs belong to Joe and Jerry, dressed as women. Jerry almost slips, asking, 'How do they walk in these things?' We cut to a **point-of-view shot** of the other girl musicians up ahead, boarding the train. Jerry gets the line, 'It's no use, we're not going to get away with this.' But just as he says this, Jerry catches sight of something that helps him see things differently – Sugar Kane. The camera moves to a close-up of Sugar's face, following her as she sassily swings along the platform. The camera cuts back to Joe and Jerry and the incredulous looks on their faces. Bursts of steam from the train blow out and Sugar does a sexy swivel to avoid it, whilst the camera, still on a medium close-up of her behind, cuts back to Jerry, who utters the immortal line, 'look at that, it's just like jello on springs.' Just as Jerry starts to doubt once again that they will be able to pull off impersonating women, the camera cuts to a newsboy walking down the platform, selling the evening paper: 'Extra, extra, read all about it! Seven slaughtered in north side garage, feared bloody aftermath!' The camera cuts back to Jerry. In the typical nervous, ironic tone we come to expect from him, he declares, 'You've talked me into it.' The scene ends with Joe and Jerry introducing themselves as 'the new girls' as they board the train. In minutes the narrative has advanced greatly; editing and cinematography have been used skilfully to achieve this.

contexts

ideological readings

When Spats and his cohorts arrive at the hotel, Joe and Jerry are forced to make a quick getaway. Daphne is sad to be deserting Osgood, and remarks, 'I tell you, I will never find another man who's so good to me.' Daphne's comment represents the traditional attitudes towards love and marriage, which are present and correct in *Some Like It Hot*. When Sugar is alone and without a man, she turns to drink – suggesting that to be single is to be unhappy. She seeks solace for her unhappiness in alcohol, where she finds comfort and a surrogate partner.

Ideologically *Some Like It Hot* upholds many of the conventional values of its day. Ideological readings are rarely straightforward, however; for instance, the film also highlights the gap between traditional 1950s attitudes and the more sexually liberated era about to begin.

No film exists in a vacuum; no commercial art does. *Some Like It Hot* is a product of popular culture, with a vast host of influences acting upon it. By examining these influences, and thereby placing the film in its true context, we can better understand the following:

- what ideological messages it contains
- how and why it was made
- what other elements of popular culture have left their mark on the film
- what influence it has had itself

As we've seen, ideological messages are contained in *Some Like It Hot* about common 1959 notions of love and marriage, whilst also

Monroe represented sex and wholesomeness

foreshadowing the sexually liberated 1960s. This dichotomy is represented in the character of Sugar. Actress Marilyn Monroe is crucial to this. For a 1950s audience, Marilyn Monroe represented sex and wholesomeness in equal measure – a duality quite common in the representation of women in films of the time. As an audience we sympathise with Sugar from the start. Her lack of success with men, drinking to forget the pain, and constantly making the same mistakes endear her to us.

Yet we are also very aware of her strong sexual presence, and we're perhaps not surprised to discover that her relationship history to date has been troubled. Marilyn Monroe's blatant sexuality, coupled with her naïve, 'dumb blonde' image, is integral to the role of Sugar and the success of the film. Her performance displays innocence in regard to her sexuality; when Junior asks Sugar how she mastered such effecting kissing techniques, she replies sweetly 'I sold kisses for the milk fund.'

The currency of *Some Like It Hot* lies in its ability to capture the attitudes of the day towards sex and marriage. Marriage was still the main goal of most women; ironically, it becomes Jerry's too. When he tells Joe that Osgood has proposed, Joe asks, 'Why would you want to marry a guy anyway?', to which the reply is, tellingly, 'Security.' In the late 1950s it would still have been the norm for most women to marry, have a family and become a housewife, whilst their husbands went out to work and provided for them.

Sugar's past relationships with men have only ever led to unhappiness – is this because she has engaged in premarital sex with them? The fact that she is purposely seeking a husband when she gets to Florida suggests that she recognises that traditional marriage, rather than casual sex, is the best option. It is not clear whether Junior and Sugar have sex on the yacht. There are none of the usual signifiers of sex that were used in films of this period – for instance, crashing waves – so we should perhaps assume that they don't. Sugar's integrity, for once, is intact.

Despite her desire to be taken seriously, and escape her carefully cultivated 'male fantasy' public image, the sexual connotations of Marilyn Monroe's image remained strong throughout her career. Yet this aspect of her persona had implications reaching beyond her role as an actor. It has even been suggested that her image was so pervasive that it actually redefined female sexuality in the 1950s; and that, as a result, women came to believe that a 'quality of desirability' (Hollows and Yankovich, 1995) was needed to make themselves and their men happy. Academic Richard Dyer suggests that Marilyn Monroe's image conforms to this notion of 'desirability', her 'blondeness and vulnerability offered a construction of female sexuality which is unthreatening and willing' (Hollows and Yankovich, 1995) (see Stars).

Ironically, Marilyn Monroe battled hard against this image. Throughout the as-yet largely conservative 1950s, she was unquestioningly consumed by the (male) audience as an object of desire. However much she tried to deny her 'sex object' image, she also recognised the benefits and advantages attached. In her now famous last interview, published just prior to her death, she explained:

> I don't mind being burdened with being glamorous and sexual ... I think that sexuality is only attractive when it is natural and spontaneous ... We are all born sexual creatures, thank God, but it's a pity so many people despise and crush this gift. I never quite understood it – this sex symbol – I always thought symbols were those things you clash together! That's the trouble, a sex symbol becomes a thing. I just hate to be a thing. But if I'm going to be a symbol of something I'd rather have it sex than some other things they've got symbols of!
>
> *Dyer, 1980*

It is worth noting, however, that Marilyn Monroe wasn't the first sexually alluring blonde in Hollywood. The Marilyn Monroe 'type' had been around since Jean Harlow first paved the way in the 1920s. Like Jean Harlow then, Marilyn Monroe offers a fascinating insight into the desires of the audiences of her times. Significantly, her first notable appearance on screen was in *The Asphalt Jungle* in 1950, the dawn of the decade; by the time of *Some Like It Hot* in 1959, her life was almost over, as too were the fifties. On screen and off, Marilyn Monroe was the foremost sex symbol of the decade. (Other blonde bombshells from this period include Jayne Mansfied, Mamie Van Doren and Brigitte Bardot.)

representations

The characters in *Some Like It Hot* are all from very similar backgrounds. The film features no black characters, no youths, and nobody with anything other than working-class roots – save a rather one-dimensional elderly millionaire. In the main, the only contrasting representations that the film offers are of men and of women. Josephine and Daphne have to go through a steep learning process to discover that being a woman isn't just about, 'second-hand wigs, a little padding here and there.' This is confirmed for them when they first set eyes on Sugar. Analysing the way she moves, Jerry exclaims, 'She must have some sort of built-in motors. I tell you, it's a whole different sex.' This difference between the sexes provides the key to the film, with the unbridled sexuality of Sugar contrasting with the repressed nature of Josephine and Daphne, who both portray a more old-fashioned type of woman. Once again, this highlights the 'old' and the 'new' perceptions of women.

Like all films, *Some Like It Hot* obviously doesn't happen in our real world; in fact, although it takes place in Chicago and Miami, 1929, it is far from an exact recreation of the real America of that time. It is not the business of *Some Like It Hot* to be a documentary. The film is closer in tone to a cartoon: with broad, larger-than-life characters and settings, it specifically represents how audiences of 1959 would have seen that era recreated in other films. So the world of the film is inhabited by pitiless gangsters, dizzy blondes, carefree millionaires and ultimately victorious lawmen.

Initially, *Some Like It Hot* makes free use of these one-dimensional characters. The audience needs easily identifiable reference points to be able to get its bearings. The opening scene alone provides all the trappings of the gangster genre: guns, police, night-time car chases and sharply dressed ne'er-do-wells. We're instantly positioned in time and space. (A caption even explicitly spells this out – 'Chicago 1929'.)

stereotypes & archetypes

In order to make us more familiar with this unfamiliar world, much use is made of archetypes – familiar character types, readily identifiable from their constant use in certain settings and situations. Soon after the opening we're in the speakeasy, with all the trappings that identify it: tap-dancers, huddled gangsters and a hopeless drunk who codedly craves 'another cup of coffee'. We meet Spats Colombo, an archetypal grim gangster boss, and his cartoonish nemesis, Federal Agent Mulligan, relentless and flippant. The point is made clearer still by the casting – Spats is played by George Raft, who regularly played humourless gangster roles, not least in *Scarface*; and Pat O'Brien appears as Mulligan – exactly the sort of role the Irish-American actor had been playing for decades (see Background: Key players' biographies). Audiences of 1959 would instantly identify these actors and recognise their character types in *Some Like It Hot*, thereby saving writers Billy Wilder and I.A.L. Diamond from wasting screen time laboriously setting up their characters.

The use of types in *Some Like It Hot* has a second purpose. As a comedy, the film's primary function is to amuse and entertain, and broad, simple characters are an easier target for jokes. In particular, **stereotypes** are often used to comic effect. Stereotypes differ from archetypes in that stereotypical characters can occur accidentally – by writers and actors relying on broad, simple traits or dialogue to colour characterisation – although the unfortunate result is a poor, lifeless character.

Racial stereotypes are used for laughs in *Some Like It Hot*: the funeral-parlour-cum-speakeasy is called 'Mozzarella's'; and musician's agent Sig Poliakoff is stereotypically Jewish, given to such cod-German exclamations as 'Schpielt sich mit der Philharmonic'. (Poliakoff's speech patterns actually owe more to Billy Wilder himself – a Jew in 1950s Hollywood – than they do to 1920s Chicago!)

With just three exceptions, every character in *Some Like It Hot* can be described in a just a few words: Sweet Sue is a prohibiting taskmaster; Poliakoff is a wisecracking agent; Osgood is a happy-go-lucky millionaire. The two gang bosses, Spats and Bonaparte, come alive in performance,

the three characters rise above their archetypal roots

but in truth there is little to differentiate them. Both are 'ruthless gangsters'.

The three exceptions are the leads – Joe, Jerry and Sugar. *Some Like It Hot* belongs to them and the other characters are functional, acting merely to populate the trio's story. On first meeting, they too appear to be archetypes: according to the screenplay, the band in the speakeasy are described as having 'been through the wringer', and Joe and Jerry are simply introduced from out of the ranks. Both are therefore earmarked as 'cynical musicians'. (To reinforce this, Joe is promptly seen to eye up a tap-dancer, and discuss with Jerry their lack of money, before suggesting they bet it on a dog.) When we met Sugar, she's caught having a covert swig of liquor, wearing a bold dress, her skirt raised. She's immediately set up as a 'good-time dumb blonde'.

But whereas their fellow characters are assigned basic traits from which they never deviate or develop, all three lead characters come to transcend their initially one-dimensional origins. Out of necessity, Joe and Jerry must dress as women and flee to Chicago; Jerry develops a strange relationship with an elderly millionaire, and Joe uses all his manipulative skills to win the heart of a woman, only to find that she still wants him when he drops all pretence. Sugar displays emotional depth through her songs, and hints at true heartache. She herself claims 'I'm not very bright', but Joe, as Josephine, counters 'I wouldn't say that'. Sugar, who en route to Miami dreams of meeting a millionaire there, falls instead for penniless Joe. The three characters rise above their archetypal roots, to change and grow.

As regards the use of more stereotypical representations of women in the film, we should bear in mind that, at the time, they were commonplace. During her career Marilyn Monroe never really got away from a narrow range of roles as the sexy, innocent, unintentionally funny blonde.

subversive meanings

Some Like It Hot contains a whole range of subversive elements. Many are intentional and functional; others are unconscious meanings. All are part and parcel of the film's effect.

subversive meanings

there is intent to this subversion

The representation of the film's setting is powerfully subversive. We see Chicago and Miami in 1929: just thirty years before the film was made, and therefore in living memory for a large section of the audience. Continued reference is made to major historical events: Prohibition, the Wall Street Crash and America's economic Depression. Gangsters are seen ferrying alcohol to speakeasies; there's murderous conflict between gangs, until one gang boss is arrested.

Yet the tone of *Some Like It Hot* is playful and comic. These events are presented as essentially humorous, albeit with a dark edge. Economic hardship and social upset are used as a backdrop to broad comedy. Real-life gangsters – hardened killers – are spoofed. In this respect *Some Like It Hot* displays a deeply subversive streak. To milk laughter from distressing events just thirty years old may be considered dark indeed.

There is intent to this subversion. The situations and character types (see Stereotypes & archetypes) would be easily recognised by American audiences in 1959. There's fun to be had in sending them up. Billy Wilder's version of Chicago is a caricature, peopled by world-weary musicians, brutal gangsters, hopeless drunks and shapely tap-dancers. It is shot in black and white and features character actors familiar from 1930s films. In this respect *Some Like It Hot* presents a comic-strip version of its setting, in a style familiar to cinema audiences of the time.

The later scenes of the film continue to subvert expectations to comic effect. Miami is shown as unnaturally different from Chicago: it is the equivalent of heaven to Chicago's hell. Miami 1929 becomes a sun-drenched paradise, where luxury and light are everywhere (see Style: Lighting). There's a millionaire with his own yacht for every girl playing on the beach (even when that girl is really a boy). It is completely free from hardship and from gangsters – initially, at least. Needless to say, the real Miami of 1929 wasn't so deliriously blissful, but there's as much comic mileage in that contrast as there is in the polar contrast to Chicago.

A major element of *Some Like It Hot* is the subversion of gender. When we first meet Joe, he manipulates and lusts after women. A short while later, he's dressed as one. Cross-dressing was far from new territory for comedy

Which of you dolls is Daphne?

Josephine and Daphne
on the bandstand

in 1959: it was being used as long ago as the seventeenth century, in Shakespeare's *Twelfth Night*. But the concept of men dressing as women was still virtually taboo for the times. For Jerry, it becomes a source of pleasure; he boards the Miami-bound train and launches gleefully into a discussion about corsets and seamstresses. For Joe, the situation proves useful too: as Josephine he casts off his masculinity and befriends Sugar as an equal, and this deeper understanding of her intensifies his desire for her.

The edge is somewhat taken off the men's enjoyment of transvestism by their ultimate need to return to their original genders. Even then, Jerry waits until the film's dying seconds to do so. It is striking, too, that some of the impact of gender role-reversal is lost by the main female character being played by a far from average woman – the sexually untamed Marilyn Monroe. (In this respect Marilyn Monroe's presence can be seen to disrupt the narrative flow of the film, see Style: Costume).

Aside from the joys of gender-swapping, *Some Like It Hot* hints at another taboo: homosexuality. It is not a common subject for late 1950s cinema, and the film never tackles it full on. Nevertheless, Osgood woos Daphne; he tangos with her and proposes marriage. Jerry declares that he craves 'security' and describes Osgood as 'dynamite' – and when Jerry admits he's a man, Osgood famously doesn't mind. In no way was homosexual behaviour the acceptable norm in 1959: in fact, the humour absolutely depends on us finding this subversion laughable. All the same, the suggestion of such behaviour is a subversive message for a film of that time to contain.

The comedy value of such behaviour doesn't quite extend to lesbianism, though. In the final scenes, as Joe flees the gangsters, he kisses Sugar whilst in full female dress. *Some Like It Hot* delights in pushing the boundaries of taste, but even Billy Wilder can't quite mine the comedy here: although it causes laughter, it is diffused by a reaction shot of Sweet Sue, speechless in shock. This is powerful stuff, in just implying a lesbian kiss.

Finally, a strong subversive streak in the film is the habit characters have of constantly seeking forbidden pleasures (see Narrative & form: Themes).

no suggestion that Jerry might be gay

Sugar craves the two things she isn't allowed – alcohol and men. She manages to get both: in one scene, she thinks she's drinking on a yacht with a multimillionaire. (In fact she's on a stranger's yacht with Joe in disguise as Junior.) In contrast to the sober Prohibition setting, the main characters of *Some Like It Hot* want to indulge themselves. Bearing in mind that this constitutes an illegal act (although Prohibition was a distant memory by 1959), this too is a complex message for the film to contain, which doesn't strictly conform to societal norms at the time audiences first saw it.

cultural contexts

Some Like It Hot is liberal in other ways too, not least in its attitude towards cross-dressing. Cross-dressing had of course been seen in cinema before, but never quite in this way. Usually male characters impersonating women in films such as *I Was A Male War Bride* (1949) had been depicted as uncomfortable and constantly aware of the ridiculousness of wearing the wrong gender's clothes. (*I Was a Male War Bride* features Cary Grant playing a French army officer who must dress up as a French woman in order to get to America and consummate his wedding. There's more than a passing resemblance in Tony Curtis's performance as Joe, who dresses up as a woman – and then dresses up as a millionaire whilst impersonating Cary Grant – especially given Tony Curtis's reverence for Cary Grant: see Background.)

Although both Joe and Jerry have reservations about dressing up as women, when they actually do – after some initial difficulties – they seem very much at home with their new selves. As Jerry first enters the train bound to Miami, finding the girls of the band all getting seated, he opens a discussion on his lack of need for a corset: 'I never wear one ... I have the most divine little seamstress that comes in once a month – and my dear, she's so inexpensive.' Yet nothing is implied about the sexuality of these two men turned women. It is taken for granted that they are heterosexual – even though we never actually see Jerry with a woman (in fact he ends up with a man). When Osgood proposes marriage, there is no suggestion that Jerry might be gay. It is also unlikely that the audience of the time would have read the film in this way, not being used to openly gay characters as we are today. A modern audience would almost certainly question Jerry's sexuality, given the turn of events (see Subversive meanings).

With its racy style of comedy, *Some Like It Hot* broke new ground. Compare a box-office hit of the same year: *Pillow Talk* (1959), starring Rock Hudson and Doris Day – another 'battle of the sexes' romantic comedy. The simple plot concerns a telephone party line, which brings the two main characters together, initially through dislike and later through love. The contemporary setting provided an opportunity to represent popular speech patterns of the day, the latest fashions and, most significantly, attitudes towards sex. The film is full of sexual innuendo, but crucially Jann Morrow (Doris Day) falls for the charms of the most eligible man in Manhattan, Brad Allen (Rock Hudson), without succumbing to him sexually. In this respect, the film presents a far more conservative version of gender relationships in 1959 than *Some Like It Hot* (even though the latter is set thirty years earlier).

As a movie icon, Doris Day also transmits strikingly different signals to those of Marilyn Monroe. Doris Day's image suggests gentle sophistication: a smart, good-hearted woman-about-town who is nevertheless without a hint of sexual threat. To audiences today, though, Doris Day's image is seen as hopelessly dated: she represents a female lifestyle from an earlier age. Marilyn Monroe's image, on the other hand, with her simple, direct sexuality, has endured timelessly.

Another significant feature of the cinema of the 1950s is nostalgia (perhaps surprisingly, given that post-Second-World-War society was enjoying an economic golden age: although the boom was at its height during the early 1950s, the latter part of the decade was still prospering). This nostalgia was due in part to the social complexities of the decade. Politically and domestically it was a time of unrest. At the start of the decade, Senator Joseph McCarthy sent a wave of paranoia through the United States: he accused members of the State Department and leading intellectuals, including playwright Arthur Miller, of being communists. (There was a move in Hollywood to convince the House Un-American

Activities Committee that the American film industry was fervently patriotic, as films such as *I Was a Communist for the FBI* (1951) testify.) The Cold War, the atomic bomb, the advent of the 'teenager', and the birth of rock and roll were other raging 'problems' throughout this period.

Yet despite the fact that there were serious political issues to deal with, the concept of 'leisure time' became a growing reality: with the post-war consumerist boom in full swing, the population on average had more money to spend, too. The entertainment system that came into its own in the 1950s was television. Ownership of television sets escalated. Suddenly it was an important aspect of people's lives, with weekly soap serials such as *Peyton Place* essential viewing – providing a pastime and a talking point for American housewives the length of the country.

In spite of the fast-developing interest in television, Americans of the 1950s still went to the cinema. Arguably, the film industry recognised the threat that television represented to it, and countered it by coming out with guns blazing. Some of the key American films of all time were made during this decade – among them *From Here to Eternity* (1953), *On The Waterfront* (1954), *Rebel Without a Cause* (1955) and *The Searchers* (1956). Billy Wilder was one of the foremost film **directors** of this period: his contribution to the significant films of the decade began at the beginning with *Sunset Boulevard* (1950); continued through *The Seven Year Itch* in the middle (1955) and concluded with *Some Like It Hot* at the decade's end (1959) (see Background: Key players' biographies).

It is of course difficult to condense and define a whole decade of cinema. Writer and critic, Andrew Sarris has said, 'the fifties were not just ducktails, chino jackets and method mumbling'. It was very much a transitional decade, and at times of change, people are wont to look back to the past for reassurance and comfort.

Some Like It Hot was very much an end-of-the-decade product, pointing towards the fact that the American public was changing and developing a taste for sophisticated entertainment. The film's racy content is a mere suggestion of things to come. By the 1960s the permissive society was here to stay and the hints of sex that Marilyn Monroe had offered in the 1950s were replaced by a frankness never seen before. Films like *The Graduate* (1967) and *Bob & Carol & Ted & Alice* (1969) gave the public what they now wanted – and what they could now accept.

social context

Some Like It Hot is set during America's Prohibition. Prohibition was born of the Volstead Act of 1919, which banned the manufacture, sale or consumption of alcohol. Needless to say, it provided criminal gangs with an opportunity to cash in on the nation's thirst. Gangs flourished as they illicitly manufactured their own alcohol – referred to as 'hooch' or 'moonshine'. They even managed hidden drinking dens, called 'speakeasies', into which chosen citizens – in the possession of appropriate passwords – would be allowed entrance, and then watch scantily clad dancing girls, listen to jazz bands, and, most essentially, partake of this 'home-made' alcohol. (In particular, the Italian-American Mafia became prime proponents of these illegal thrills.)

In their role as prime thirst-quenchers to the nation, criminals became immensely popular public figures. A popularity poll carried out in 1931 revealed that only film stars were above gangsters in the nation's affections. Real-life gangsters found further exposure in the movies of the day, when played on screen by the likes of actors James Cagney and Edward G. Robinson. By the time Prohibition ended in 1933, Al Capone – one of the nation's favourite gangsters – was in prison on a charge of tax evasion. By then, America was suffering further with the economic Depression, caused by the Wall Street stock-market crash of 1929.

Despite the grim reality of life in the 1920s and 1930s, *Some Like It Hot* represents blatant nostalgia for this earlier era. Not insignificantly, the gangster serial *The Untouchables* was one of the most popular shows on television in 1959. *Some Like It Hot* exploits this rather dark obsession, beginning as it does with a mass murder and containing several other gangster killings along the way. Nostalgia also plays a part in the way the film spoofs old movie clichés: Spats's arch-enemy Little Bonaparte (Nehemiah Persoff) apes Edward G. Robinson's most famous characterisation as Rico Bandello in *Little Caesar* (1930).

intertextuality

The film also contains all manner of inside movie in-jokes. Edward G. Robinson and George Raft were originally cast as the chief gangsters, but they had famously fallen out in 1941 whilst working together on *Manpower*, with Edward G. Robinson declaring that he would never work with George Raft again. Although Edward G. Robinson withdrew from the project, *Some Like It Hot* nevertheless features his son, Edward G. Robinson Junior. (According to legend, Robinson Junior was very poor in even this tiny part: and director Billy Wilder was furious, having agreed to cast him as a favour to his father, only to lose Robinson Senior from the cast.) When Spats (played by George Raft) arrives at the Hotel Seminole Ritz for the Italian gangster convention, Robinson Junior appears as the gangster flipping a coin. Spats grabs the coin, saying 'Where'd you learn a cheap trick like that?' This is an in-joke reference to the identical habit of the Raft character in *Scarface*.

genre

The concept of genre criticism emerged in the mid 1960s. In terms of how the film industry had historically organised and marketed itself, though, genre had always been in operation, as a means of helping viewers identify the type of film they wanted to see. Each genre, be it the western, romantic comedy, or science fiction, has its own set of conventions covering everything from the style of musical score to the choice of stars, setting and plot.

The flexibility of genres is evidenced by their ability to cross-breed: for instance, cinema has produced the sci-fi horror film (*Alien*, 1979) and the musical western (*Annie Get Your Gun*, 1950). *Some Like It Hot* blends the gangster movie, slapstick comedy, romance and a dash of music to produce a hybrid with wide audience appeal.

Until the emergence of genre theory, writing on the gangster movie took two main points of view: the censorial (that is, castigating such films and their makers for depicting such unseemly subject matter), or the journalistic (graphic background accounts of the real-life crime upon

the classic gangster film was cheap to make

which the films were based). Gangster films often came ripped straight from the nation's front-page stories, and this caused problems for early genre criticism relating to the films: they were too closely related to the contemporary events they fictionalised.

This ability to better represent 'true life' created a market for true-life stories (not to mention the audiences' desire to sample such novelties). Just as Hollywood moved away from fantasy to reality-based cinema, lurid accounts of gangster violence dominated the newspapers of the day.

The gangster film emerged as a distinct genre in the 1930s. A major factor was the development of sound cinema. It added a whole new element to film-making, which allowed a film more closely to resemble 'real life' – that is, it coupled images with sound. Free from the restrictions of using images alone, cinema could now move away from being a purely photographic enterprise, and feature moving, talking images. The classic gangster film was cheap to make. It was possible to use near-contemporary dress, and suitable existing settings – such as real restaurants and hotel rooms – with exteriors usually being shot on studio back-lots. In his study guide on the gangster film Tom Ryall divides iconographic elements of the gangster genre into:

- the physical presence, attributes and dress of the actors and characters they play
- the urban milieu in which the fiction is played out
- the technology at the gangsters' disposal

The fast-action pace made them excellent thrillers, and critics were even prepared to defend them against censorious religious pressure groups. Warner Brothers cleverly found a way of mollifying the protesters whilst keeping the thrills coming: they made the policeman into the hero, in films such as *Bullets or Ballots* (1936). In 1931 James Cagney made *The Public Enemy*, a drab, low-key film which points to the sadness and deprivation of big-city life as the cause of crime. By 1939, the heat of criticism had cooled sufficiently to enable production to go ahead on *The Roaring Twenties* (1939) – one of the most violent films of the whole genre. In later times, when nostalgia set in, films were made which parodied this glut of

1930s gangster films – just as *Some Like It Hot* does so successfully.

Although *Some Like It Hot* spoofs the gangster genre, its true nature is as a 1950s comedy. Big-screen comedy changed markedly during this decade, from animal-based capers such as the *Francis* series of films featuring a talking mule, and *Harvey* (1950), starring James Stewart and a six-foot rabbit; to the more grown-up *Roman Holiday* (1953) starring Audrey Hepburn. Compared to most 1950s comedies, *Some Like It Hot* marked new territory in its sophistication. The original trailer tells us, 'Not since the Marx Brothers so much comedy', leading the audience to expect slapstick, wisecracking and absurdity. Yet it is not all knockabout farce. The film also had a complexity which audiences responded to. The Wall Street Crash of 1929 signalled the start of the Depression, a low point in American history; Billy Wilder and I.A.L. Diamond use these relatively recent events as a vehicle for humour. Those watching *Some Like It Hot* in 1959 were laughing at something which, up until that point, would have been a painful memory.

The success of *Some Like It Hot* as a comedy lies initially with the sharp, witty dialogue of Billy Wilder and I.A.L. Diamond's script. However, it is the delivery by the film's great acting talents that brings the comedy out. And whilst Tony Curtis and Jack Lemmon perform wonderfully, it is perhaps Marilyn Monroe who surprises us most. Although known primarily throughout her career as a 'dumb blonde', Marilyn Monroe was undoubtedly a gifted comic, contributing greatly to some of the decade's most memorable comedies, including *How To Marry a Millionaire* and *Gentlemen Prefer Blondes*. In the two films she made with Billy Wilder – *The Seven Year Itch* and *Some Like It Hot* – her natural comic talent shines through.

production

The golden age of Hollywood formally began in 1913, when Cecil B. De Mille made a film for a number of investors who would later form Paramount Pictures. From this period on, a system known as vertical integration operated, whereby just a few major companies – the five biggest were Paramount, Twentieth Century Fox, MGM, Warner Brothers and RKO – produced, distributed and exhibited their own movies. By owning the best movie theatres in the biggest cities, they had a stranglehold on the market.

This system continued for quite some time; immediately after the Second World War, the situation finally began to change. Factors included the declining size of cinema audiences, the rise of television and increased competition from foreign films, but the biggest challenge to the domination of the major studios came from the US government. The strength of the majors was eventually broken when the government ruled that production and distribution had to be separated from exhibition. Despite the studios' appeal against this legislation, the market was opened up from 1948.

The end of this golden age had a profound effect on all the studios, and United Artists – who provided the financial backing for *Some Like It Hot* – entered the 1950s in financial dire straits. The company's founders, Charlie Chaplin and Mary Pickford, sold the business to a couple of entertainment lawyers from New York. The timing was ripe for the two young hotshots to bring in independent production. John Huston, Otto Preminger and Billy Wilder were just three of the directors they began to work with. Without studio overheads – i.e. running a studio plant, and paying the wages of the stars under contract – they could concentrate on making movies and making money.

One major drawback to the demise of the studio system was that high-quality technicians who were assigned to particular studios went freelance, and it became more difficult to put a skilled team of people together to make a film. However, this was a small price to pay in the face of the new creative freedom. United Artists began simply to provide financing and distribution for independent producers. As a much smaller company than their competitors Paramount and Warners, they adapted easily to working in this more flexible manner. A new era of deal-making followed, and new kinds of contracts with single- or multiple-picture deals were devised for producers.

Some Like It Hot was made during October 1958. The Goldwyn studios in Hollywood were hired for the Chicago scenes and all the interior work. The exterior scenes were shot on location in nearby San Diego, which stands in for Florida. (This has been identified as an error in the film – since the landscape of Florida is flat, and certainly doesn't feature the like of the California hills seen in the background.) The 'Seminole Ritz' Hotel was, in fact, San Diego's Hotel Coronado del Mar.

The film's production company, Mirisch, was formed by the four brothers Mirisch, who broke away from Allied Artists studios to form their own concern. As befitted the creative freedom of the times, Mirisch's contract with Billy Wilder allowed him free range in casting, choice of screenplay and even choice of subject. He received final cut – and thus final control over content of the released film – and a twenty-five per cent share of profit. (The stars of *Some Like It Hot* also received a percentage share of profits.) The ownership of the film resembles a family tree: made for United Artists by Mirisch, the film declares itself to be 'an Ashton picture – a Mirisch Company' – Ashton being Billy Wilder's private production company, a further subsidiary of Mirisch!

Some Like It Hot became one of the biggest grossing comedies of all time, making a great deal of money for Billy Wilder, Mirisch Pictures – and, of course, United Artists. It stands as a sterling example of the creative boom that followed the collapse of the studio system.

marketing

In the world of the late 1950s, cinema was still a relatively new industry, and the vast marketing machine with which we are now familiar was not in place. After the initial duration of a film's run, it would become difficult to see it. Home video technology was decades away, and television was just beginning to show feature films, and then only selectively. Film studios therefore had low expectations of the shelf-life of their product, and the efforts they made to market films were less thorough than is common today.

No commercial merchandising was used to promote *Some Like It Hot*; no T-shirts, postcards or mugs. In the manner of the times, the one marketing tool used was a standard two-minute theatrical trailer, shown to cinema

Marilyn Monroe is forefronted

audiences of the time. This theatrical trailer signals one element above all others: Marilyn Monroe. She dominates almost every shot, including the first and the last. With the film's jazz score playing, a shot of Marilyn Monroe, as Sugar Kane, opens the trailer. Marilyn Monroe's top billing is superimposed, followed by the film's title: another image of Marilyn Monroe appears within the O of 'Hot'.

Tony Curtis and Jack Lemmon are then introduced, quickly and in the same shot. Images of gangsters and machine-guns give us the setting for the film and the genre trappings. The voice-over promises: 'Not since *Scarface* so much action. Not since the Marx Brothers so much comedy. Not since *The Seven Year Itch* so much Marilyn!', this last phrase coming over Sugar's celebrated entrance-wiggle on the train platform. (It goes without saying that Marilyn Monroe is presented as the main attraction. Indeed, she need only be referred to by her first name.)

The voice-over goes on to claim, 'You've never laughed so much at sex – or a picture about it!' before the three stars are billed again, Marilyn first and boldest. Titles then read 'The most comedy ever! The biggest comedy ever! The hottest comedy ever!' The musical backing includes an orchestral version of 'I Wanna Be Loved By You'. As it comes to an end the trailer even plugs the United Artists soundtrack album – 'Hear Marilyn sing the fabulous songs of the Roaring Twenties!' and ends with Marilyn Monroe as Sugar Kane performing 'Running Wild' with the band. (Jack Lemmon subsequently followed Marilyn Monroe's lead and in 1959 he recorded *Jack Lemmon Plays and Sings Music From Some Like It Hot*, featuring 1920s standards, as his second album for Epic Records.) At the trailer's end the film's title shows once more: and beneath, in tiny billing, we discover this is 'A Billy Wilder Production'. (Of course, Billy Wilder is arguably the individual most responsible for the entire film.)

The trailer pushes three features to prospective audiences. First and foremost, this is a Marilyn Monroe film. It is also a comedy, and it is about sex. That Marilyn Monroe is forefronted is no surprise. She was a premier star in 1959, and she hadn't been seen on screen since *The Prince and the Showgirl* two years earlier. Her next film, *Let's Make Love* (1960), was another year away. For Marilyn Monroe fans – and that meant nearly everyone – *Some Like It Hot* was a major event.

Despite her best efforts to improve her stock as a serious actor, she was still best known as a comedy star, and therefore marketing *Some Like It Hot* as a Marilyn Monroe comedy – as the trailer does – is a sure-fire way of appealing to the late 1950s film-goer. The trailer doesn't promise a profound or challenging experience. It promises laughs and relentless entertainment for a wide audience.

Curiously though, it also promises 'sex' – the images of a pouting, dancing, wiggling Marilyn Monroe tell us so: so too does the voice-over, explicitly and in so many words. On the film's release, the swinging sixties were just around the corner and sex as a subject for popular culture would become much more acceptable. Nevertheless, America in 1959 was a far from liberal place, and the boldness with which the trailer promises we will 'laugh at sex' is remarkable. In that respect this is the most pertinent point the trailer makes about the finished film. *Some Like It Hot* is hard to describe as simply a 'Marilyn Monroe Sex Comedy' – but the sexual content of the film is strong for the time. (Interestingly, the trailer tempts audiences with talk of sex – forbidden pleasure – just as characters in the film are constantly seeking their own forbidden pleasure, see Narrative & form.)

Other than the trailer, no major marketing techniques were employed to promote the film, although it nevertheless became a huge hit. The record albums by Marilyn Monroe and Jack Lemmon were released in 1959 – but this is in the context that both characters play musicians, that 1920s songs were repeatedly used within the film and suggested within Adolph Deutsch's score, and that both stars had previously released other albums of songs. This doesn't equate to modern use of soundtracks as a marketing tool, when hit singles can cross-promote the film. Instead it represents, at worst, opportunism on the part of those stars. In the following year's *Pepe* (1960), the actor Cantinflas stars as a Mexican scouring Hollywood in search of his pet horse. In the manner of a variety show, his escapades involve a horde of star names in cameo roles. Jack Lemmon appears in a brief sequence, confusing the Mexican by changing in and out of a familiar

publicity

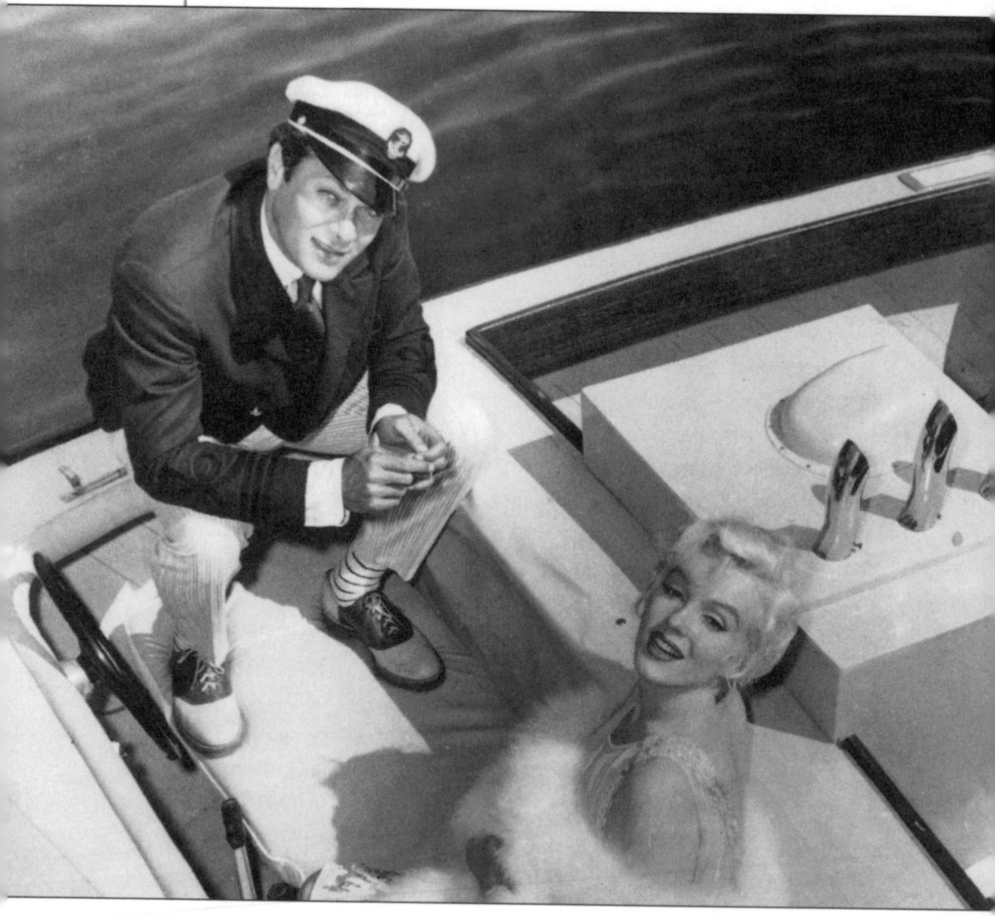

Publicity shot of
Marilyn Monroe and Tony Curtis
for *Some Like It Hot*

dress. This uncredited reappearance of Daphne, so soon after the release of *Some Like It Hot*, might be seen as movie cross-marketing; otherwise, it is simply a fond tribute to a well-loved film character.

stars

Film stars have been a source of fascination since cinema began. However, as interest in stars and stardom is very much a popular pastime, studying them has been made difficult. Our personal feelings and obsessions about our favourite stars obfuscate theoretical study.

The main objective of star theory has been to discover why stars are popular. It recognises that stars are the product of a whole series of texts aside from the film – including promotional publicity such as posters, trailers and interviews, and serious film criticism. By bringing together on-screen appearances with a star's off-screen real life, we start to build up a more complete picture of the star's image. Marilyn Monroe first became known to the public through an early series of pin-ups (See Background: Key players' biographies), and continued to receive exposure throughout her life, through her films, articles about her private life, interviews and photographs. Her public and private personas often mesh into one entity in the eyes of the majority of the public. Academic Richard Dyer claims that Marilyn Monroe had a symbolic relationship with Hollywood:

> she represented those who believed or loved Hollywood's dreams, the conflict between its glamour and the desire for an ordinary (married) life, and the destructive force of the Hollywood machine or dream-factory.
>
> *Dyer, 1980*

There is still an overwhelming public and critical desire to deconstruct Marilyn Monroe – both her public and private selves – and to understand the tragedy of this young woman who seemingly couldn't cope with her own stardom. Yet it is precisely because of the contradictory nature of her stardom that she has remained in the public consciousness for so long.

sex appeal and timing

Some Like It Hot is a Marilyn Monroe star vehicle. Her star presence alone would have been sufficient to draw an audience to see the film. The fact that she doesn't sing or dance very well is irrelevant. Marilyn is decidedly the film's main draw.

Ironically, Marilyn Monroe herself confided to friends that she felt her role to be as a 'straight man' to Tony Curtis and Jack Lemmon. In fact, her performance won her the best critical notices of her career. For critics, the only question was the degree to which Marilyn Monroe was acting – or appearing as herself? Of course, the truth lies somewhere between the two. The power of her performance lies in her ability to fashion a comic character and simultaneously allow her natural charisma to shine. It is this ability that her fans unquestioningly understood, and that makes her such an enduring star.

reception

At a sneak preview of *Some Like It Hot* in December 1958 held at the Bay Theatre, Pacific Palisades, California, audiences sat watching the film in mirthless silence. Further previews were held at Loews Lexington cinema in New York. Here on the other side of America, the reception was rapturous; Marilyn Monroe was ferried away in a limousine as the frenziedly happy audience mobbed her.

The latter reaction was much more representative of the general public's appreciation of the film when it was released in March 1959. The critics loved the film and they adored Marilyn Monroe in it. By spoofing the dumb blonde image that had made her so famous, she had finally won the critics' approval. *Variety* hailed her as 'a comedienne with that combination of sex appeal and timing that just can't be beat'. Oddly, Marilyn Monroe's husband Arthur Miller was dismissive of the film. Having encouraged her to accept the project, he declared Sugar to be 'a tasteless and characterless ingenue which [Marilyn] had to invest with some life so that it was real ... she had made something out of nothing'. Arthur Miller despatched aggressive messages to Billy Wilder, even blaming the making of the film for her losing their baby. (see Background: Key players' biographies). Thankfully, Arthur Miller was present at the New York preview. Seeing the film in its entirety for the first time, amongst a positively delighted audience, he decided the result was, after all, something special.

Some Like It Hot has everything that film-goers of the time wanted: comedy and farce, thriller elements and plenty of sexual innuendo. Astonishingly just one Academy Award was forthcoming despite all the talents at peak form on show. Audiences nevertheless packed out the movie theatres, and the film still ranks as one of the highest grossing comedies ever made.

The following year, Billy Wilder directed *The Apartment*, written with I.A.L. Diamond, starring Jack Lemmon and made for Mirisch Pictures. This time three Academy Awards winged their way home with Billy Wilder. In 1959 Tony Curtis made the wartime comedy drama *Operation Petticoat*, starring alongside his inspiration and idol, Cary Grant; and Marilyn Monroe reprised her blonde male-fantasy persona in *Let's Make Love*. Her career, and her life, ended two years later.

bibliography

Altman – Nowell-Smith

general film

Altman, Rick, *Film Genre,*
BFI, 1999
Detailed exploration of film genres

Bordwell, David, *Narration in the Fiction Film,* Routledge, 1985
A detailed study of narrative theory and structures

– – –, Staiger, Janet & Thompson, Kristin, *The Classical Hollywood Cinema: Film Style & Mode of Production to 1960,* Routledge, 1985; pbk 1995
An authoritative study of cinema as institution, it covers film style and production

– – – & Thompson, Kristin, *Film Art,*
McGraw-Hill, 4th edn, 1993
An introduction to film aesthetics for the non-specialist

Branson, Gill & Stafford, Roy, *The Media Studies Handbook,* Routledge, 1996

Buckland, Warren, *Teach Yourself Film Studies,* Hodder & Stoughton, 1998
Very accessible, it gives an overview of key areas in film studies

Cook, Pam (ed.), *The Cinema Book,*
BFI, 1994

Corrigan, Tim, *A Short Guide To Writing About Film,*
HarperCollins, 1994
What it says: a practical guide for students

Dyer, Richard, *Stars,* BFI, 1979;
pbk Indiana University Press, 1998
A good introduction to the star system

Easthope, Antony, *Classical Film Theory,* Longman, 1993
A clear overview of recent writing about film theory

Hayward, Susan, *Key Concepts in Cinema Studies,*
Routledge, 1996

Hill, John & Gibson, Pamela Church (eds), *The Oxford Guide to Film Studies,*
Oxford University Press, 1998
Wide-ranging standard guide

Lapsley, Robert & Westlake, Michael, *Film Theory: An Introduction,*
Manchester University Press, 1994

Maltby, Richard & Craven, Ian, *Hollywood Cinema,*
Blackwell, 1995
A comprehensive work on the Hollywood industry and its products

Mulvey, Laura, 'Visual Pleasure and Narrative Cinema' (1974), in Visual and Other Pleasures,
Indiana University Press, Bloomington, 1989
The classic analysis of 'the look' and 'the male gaze' in Hollywood cinema. Also available in numerous other edited collections

Nelmes, Jill (ed.), *Introduction to Film Studies,*
Routledge, 1996
Deals with several national cinemas and key concepts in film study

Nowell-Smith, Geoffrey (ed.), *The Oxford History of World Cinema,*
Oxford University Press, 1996
Hugely detailed and wide-ranging with many features on 'stars'

Thomson, David, ***A Biographical Dictionary of the Cinema,***
Secker & Warburg, 1975
Unashamedly driven by personal taste, but often stimulating

Truffaut, François, ***Hitchcock,***
Simon & Schuster, 1966,
rev. edn, Touchstone, 1985
Landmark extended interview

Turner, Graeme, ***Film as Social Practice,*** 2nd edn, Routledge, 1993
Chapter four, 'Film Narrative', discusses structuralist theories of narrative

Wollen, Peter, ***Signs and Meaning in the Cinema,***
Viking, 1972
An important study in semiology

Readers should also explore the many relevant websites and journals. *Film Education* and *Sight and Sound* are standard reading.

Valuable websites include:

The Internet Movie Database at
http://uk.imdb.com

Screensite at
http://www.tcf.ua.edu/screensite/contents.html

The Media and Communications Site at the University of Aberystwyth at
http://www.aber.ac.uk/~dgc/welcome.html

There are obviously many other university and studio websites which are worth exploring in relation to film studies.

some like it hot

Baltake, Joe, ***Jack Lemmon: His Films and Career,***
Columbus Books, 1986

Brode, Douglas,
The Films of The Fifties,
Carol Publishing Group, 1992

Cousins, Mark, (Introduction to)
The Apartment (screenplay),
Faber and Faber, 1988

Crowe, Cameron,
Conversations with Wilder,
Faber and Faber, 1999

Curtis, Tony, and Paris, Barry,
Tony Curtis: The Autobiography,
Heinemann, 1994

Dyer, Richard, ***Marilyn Monroe: Star Dossier One,*** BFI, 1980

Guiles, Fred Lawrence,
Norma Jean: The Life and Death of Marilyn Monroe,
Grafton Books, 1986

Hollows, J., and Yankovich, M., (eds)
Approaches to Popular Film,
MU Press, 1995

Pirie, David,
Anatomy of the Movies,
Windward, 1981

Sarris, Andrew,
Politics and Cinema,
Columbia University Press, 1978

Summers, Anthony,
Goddess: The Secret Lives of Marilyn Monroe,
Sphere Books Limited, 1985

cinematic terms

antagonist the main character's opponent: the film's villain. If the protagonist is said to be on some kind of 'quest', the antagonist is the character placing obstacles in his or her path

auteur literally the 'author' of the film. An auteur has a strong individual style and favoured themes, and is the chief creative force within the film. A director of note may be tagged 'auteur', implying their vision is paramount. Occasionally, a strong screenwriter or even actor, might be called an 'auteur'

cinematographer essentially the role liaising between the director and the camera operators. The cinematographer is responsible for translating the director's conception of shots into actual camerawork. Noted cinematographers can have an impact on the look of a film on screen equal to – or even greater than – the director's

cinematography the basic term for 'cinema photography' – any treatment of the physical film image, be it during filming or during laboratory developing

closure a film's narrative can be said to have reached full closure when all strands of the narrative have been tied up at the conclusion. Alternatively, events may have been set into motion that haven't been seen through to their conclusion, and closure is thereby only partial

cut the immediate linking of two shots within a film

diegesis all elements within the world of the frame, including characters, props and sound

director the individual responsible for overseeing the shooting, deciding which shots to film, and liaising with cast and crew. The importance of the role can change – 'second unit' directors might shoot secondary scenes, and the director need not always be involved in editing – but the director is ultimately in charge of getting the screenplay on film

dissolve less immediate than a cut, in a dissolve two images are blended together as the first 'dissolves' and the second appears

editing the post-production of joining together selected shots by cuts, fades or wipes, to create the seamless flow of the film's narrative. A good deal of a film's ultimate effect can be created through well-judged editing, and a director will therefore usually be closely involved

fade a shot gradually appearing from – or disappearing to – a blank screen

frame the shaped image on screen, making use of objects and actors, most often composed by the director

genre a type of film identifiable by recurrent use of conventions – such a science-fiction, horror or action film

mise-en-scène the chosen contents of the frame, from sets and props to actors and special effects

motif any element that recurs in a film to cumulative effect, relating to a theme. It may be sound, an image or a setting. By way of example, *Don't Look Now* (1973) makes repeated use of the colour red, and images of water

narration the gradual exposition of the film's story through the plot. This can take various forms – from a first-person spoken narration, restricted by the amount the narrator-character knows of the story; to a less blatant, yet omniscient narration via the film-maker's invisible guidance of the plot

pan a horizontal movement of the film image, created by the camera operator turning the camera to point to one side

plot the sequence of events shown within a film. This need not follow the chronological story

point-of-view shot (or P.O.V.) a shot replicating a character's own field of vision within the frame

producer responsible for creating and setting up a film production. Whereas the director oversees the hands-on filming, the producer takes charge of more executive, often financial matters pertaining to a film, and usually has less of a creative role

protagonist the main character in the film. Most stories can be seen a some kind of quest. The protagonist is therefore the character whose quest the film depicts

screenplay the initial script of the film, featuring directions, descriptions and dialogue, laid out to a set format. May differ from the finished film should changes be made during shooting

shot a single image – be it mobile or static – within a film, completed by a cut. Certain standard shot sizes are best described in terms of how a human figure is framed – long shot: a full standing figure; medium close-up: head to chest of a figure; close-up: head, and perhaps shoulders, of a figure; extreme (or big) close-up: the face only, or a single expression

space the physical space between objects in a shot. Space could only be given proper consideration once lenses became available that could lend three-dimensional depth of field to a shot, by allowing objects in the background to be in sharp focus at the same time as the foreground being focused. Hence in *Citizen Kane* (1941), when characters move from the foreground to the background of a shot, this represents their lessened importance

stereotype an oversimplified, one-dimensional character, identifiable by certain characteristics – such as a 'mousy housewife' or a 'brash American'. Most often either a deliberate target for ridicule, or else the result of poorly developed writing or acting

story the chronological sequence of events touched on within a film. However, the film follows a plot, and the sequence may be altered, or events simply not shown

studio system large film studios, specialising in large-scale production over the long term, contracting staff – from technicians through to big-name actors and directors – and hence producing films almost entirely 'in-house'. More prevalent in Hollywood in an earlier era: production since the 1950s became increasingly independent. Nevertheless, the system still exists, on a smaller scale, today

take a single, uninterrupted run of film in a camera. Several takes may be made of a single scene, and one take selected to form the actual shot in the finished film

wipe a less immediate cut, where the second cut moves into the frame, covering the first

credits

director

Billy Wilder

producer

Billy Wilder

screenplay

Billy Wilder and I.A.L. Diamond

cinematographer

Charles Lang

film editing

Arthur P. Schmidt

original music

Adolph Deutsch

costume

Orry Kelly

editor

Doane Harrison

cast

Sugar Kane – Marilyn Monroe

Joe – Tony Curtis

Jerry – Jack Lemmon

Osgood Fielding III – Joe E. Brown

Spats Colombo – George Raft

Mulligan – Pat O'Brien

Sweet Sue – Joan Shawlee

Sig Poliakoff – Billy Gray

Bonaparte – Nehemiah Persoff

Bienstock – Dave Barry